Second Edition

Culturally Speaking

A Conversation and Culture Text

Rhona B. Genzel

Rochester Institute of Technology
English Language Center

Martha Graves Cummings

Drury College
Springfield, Missouri

HEINLE & HEINLE PUBLISHERS
A Division of Wadsworth, Inc.
Boston, Massachusetts 02116 USA

AG

To our families, who contributed and continue to contribute to our culture, and who taught us to appreciate, respect, and enjoy the cultures of others.

The publication of *Culturally Speaking,* Second Edition, was directed by the members of the Newbury House Publishing Team at Heinle & Heinle:

Erik Gundersen, Editorial Director
Gabrielle B. McDonald, Production Editor

Also participating in the publication of this program were:

Publisher: Stanley J. Galek
Editorial Production Manager: Elizabeth Holthaus
Project Manager: Hockett Editorial Service
Assistant Editor: Karen P. Hazar
Associate Marketing Manager: Donna Hamilton
Production Assistant: Maryellen Eschmann
Manufacturing Coordinator: Mary Beth Lynch
Photo Coordinator: Martha Leibs-Heckly
Illustrator: Brian Orr
Interior Designer: Rita Naughton
Cover Illustrator and Designer: Brooke Scudder

Photo credits (page numbers are given in boldface type): 10—United Press International; 11—AP/Wide World; 12–15, 17–22—Carol Palmer; 27—H. Dratch, The Image Works; 46A, C—Michael LaJoie; 46 B, D, E, 109 B—Martha Graves Cummings; 47 F—Peter Simon, Stock, Boston; 47 G—Bettye Lane, Photo Researchers; 49—Rhoda Sidney, The Image Works; 59—Steve and Mary Skjold; 81—Mitch Wojnarowicz, The Image Works; 83—Roberta Hershenson, Photo Researchers; 84, 150 bottom right—Barbara Alper, Stock, Boston; 90 top left—Larry Kolvoord, The Image Works; 90 top right—John Griffin, The Image Works; 90 bottom left—Michael Dwyer, Stock, Boston; 90 bottom right, 92 right—Four By Five; 92 left—Dion Ogust, The Image Works; 95A, 109A—Barbara Rios, Photo Researchers; 95B—J. Berndt, Stock, Boston; 96—Herwig, Stock, Boston; 109C—Frances M. Cox, Stock, Boston; 109D—Hanna Schreiber, Photo Researchers; 110—Superstock; 118 top—Carini, The Image Works; 118 bottom—Mark Antman, The Image Works; 119—Gale Zucker, Stock, Boston; 126 left—M.B. Duda, Photo Researchers; 126 right—Beringer/Dratch, The Image Works; 128 top—Donald Dietz, Stock, Boston; 128 bottom—Rafael Macia, Photo Researchers; 150 top left—John Coletti, Stock, Boston; 150 top right—John Eastcott, Yva Momatiuk, The Image Works; 150 bottom left—David Hathcox; 167 top left—Blair Seitz, Photo Researchers; 167 top right—Harriet Gans, The Image Works; 167 bottom left—John Griffin, The Image Works; 167 bottom right—Ulrike Welsch, U Med-W/P

Heinle & Heinle Publishers is a division of Wadsworth, Inc.
Manufactured in the United States of America

Library of Congress Cataloging-in-Publication Data
Genzel, Rhona B.
    Culturally Speaking: a conversation and culture text / Rhona B.
Genzel and Martha Graves Cummings.
        p.   cm.
        ISBN 0-8384-4213-7
        1. English language—Textbooks for foreign speakers. 2. English language—Conversation and phrase books.   I. Cummings, Martha Graves. II. Title.
PE1128.G37   1993
428.3'4—dc20   93–38189
                                                                                                                    CIP

10 9 8 7 6 5 4 3 2

Contents

Overview   *vii*

To the Teacher   *ix*

Chapter One   Getting Along with People   1

1. Introductions   *2*
2. Small Talk   *5*
3. Distance and Space Requirements   *8*
4. Hand Gestures   *10*
5. Facial Gestures   *19*
6. Summary   *23*

Chapter Two   Attending School   27

1. Learning About North American Schools   *28*
2. Rules for Attending School   *31*
3. Asking for Help   *36*
4. Summary   *39*

Chapter Three   Building Friendships   43

1. Friendships Across Cultures   *43*
2. Image   *46*
3. Sharing Good and Bad Times   *48*
4. Problem Situations   *50*
5. Summary   *52*

Chapter Four   **Dating**   *58*

   1. Dating Across Cultures   *58*
   2. Dating Customs   *62*
   3. Compliments and Conversation   *65*
   4. Summary   *67*

Chapter Five   **Sharing Common Interests**   *70*

   1. North American Humor   *70*
   2. Superstitions   *76*
   3. Telling "Ghost Stories"   *80*
   4. Attitudes Toward Wild Animals and Pets   *83*
   5. Debate Over Endangered Species   *86*
   6. Health   *88*
   7. Music   *92*

Chapter Six   **Participating in Social Events**   *94*

   1. Social Events   *96*
   2. Saying the Right Thing at Weddings and Funerals   *99*
   3. Celebrating Holidays and Special Events   *101*
   4. Going Out With Friends   *111*
   5. The Concept of Time   *115*
   6. Dining Out with Friends   *118*
   7. Summary   *123*

Chapter Seven   **Shopping**   *126*

   1. Places to Shop   *127*
   2. Making Your Purchase   *131*
   3. Talking with Salespeople   *134*
   4. Problems and Solutions   *137*
   5. Summary   *141*

Chapter Eight   **Using the Telephone**   *143*

   1. Learning About the Telephone   *143*
   2. Talking on the Telephone   *146*
   3. Business and Social Uses of the Telephone   *149*
   4. Using the Directory   *151*
   5. Exploring North America   *153*
   6. Special Uses of the Telephone   *157*
   7. Summary   *159*

Chapter Nine   **Going to the Doctor**   *162*

   1. Preparing for a Visit to the Doctor   *162*
   2. Visiting the Doctor   *170*
   3. Summary   *173*

Answers   *177*
Glossary   *186*

Acknowledgments

Special thanks go to Kathryn Bonnez, Susan Unher, and Ann Gleason, who offered suggestions and shared student input with us as we prepared the second edition of *Culturally Speaking*.

We are grateful to the following instructors who reviewed *Culturally Speaking* at various stages of development and who offered many helpful insights and suggestions: Irene McKay, George Brown College of Applied Arts & Technology, Toronto; Peggy Armstrong, University of South Florida; Gail Chabran, Rio Hondo College (CA); Dee Christoffers, California State University, Fullerton; Leslie J. Bishop and Marcia Dantas-Whitney, Oregon State University; Michael Feldman, Harvard University; Martha Day, Richard Bland College (VA); Mark D. Rentz, Arizona State University; and Mary W. Herbert, University of California, Davis.

Of course, no effort could be completed without the support of our families. Rhona would like to thank her husband, George, for his encouragement and her parents who cleared the "desk" in Florida so that she could spread out and work uninterrupted during her winter vacations to their home. She would also like to thank Wendy and Willie Sherman, who shared anecdotes and articles about cross-cultural problems, some of which found their way into the text.

Overview

The second edition of *Culturally Speaking* provides more information, more exercises, and more opportunities to practice what is learned. The new book expands many of the popular sections and adds a new dimension through three new activities: *What's Going On Here?*, *Exploring North America*, and *Speaking Out*. In this edition, we are using the terms *North America* and *North American* to refer to the United States and Canada.

In *What's Going On Here?* students have an opportunity to read about a cultural misunderstanding and to discuss its cause. The *Exploring North America* section encourages students to go outside the classroom to conduct polls, allowing English-speaking members of the community to become cultural informants. In *Speaking Out* students are given opportunities to discuss controversial topical and cultural issues. The addition of these three sections heightens the importance of learning culture as a part of language learning and encourages students to interact with each other in class and with others outside of class.

We have maintained the playfulness, and exploratory nature of the book while at the same time adding opportunities for serious discussion on topics such as AIDS, the environment, and health issues like diet, smoking, and exercise.

The popular chapter on gestures (chapter 1) has been expanded to cover many more facial and hand gestures, complete with photographs and explanations. Chapters 2, 3, 4, 6, and 9 remain the same except for the addition of the three new sections. Chapter 5 has been expanded to include a ghost story, a discussion about the environment, health issues, and additional jokes.

Chapter 7 includes information about shopping with coupons, understanding advertisements, and using credit cards. Chapter 8 includes information about 800 and 900 numbers, special telephone features, and telephone and computerized surveys.

To the Teacher

The second edition of *Culturally Speaking* adds information and activities which contribute to the goal of getting students talking and acting comfortably. Each chapter focuses on a different aspect of mainstream North American culture. Students begin by making cultural comparisons and sharing information about their culture; they move on to model conversations, half dialogues, and role-plays. As students complete each chapter, they become more and more proficient, not only in the language but also in the cultural context in which language is used. They become proficient with a variety of situations and self-confident about their ability to communicate.

To help students accomplish this, each chapter contains a variety of creative exercises to spark their interest in culture and to provide them with the conversational and cultural tools they need to communicate effectively. Some of the activities included in the book and suggested methods of use are listed here.

A cassette tape which accompanies the text allows students to listen to conversational English in order to discover how words and idioms are pronounced and how inflection is used to convey meaning.

Let's Share
Let's Share is designed to encourage discussion on a topic that students are uniquely qualified to discuss—their country and its customs. Students enjoy this exercise because they know the content well and are eager to share information about their culture with others. Therefore, in addition to teaching cultural elements, it fosters lively discussions. The atmosphere should reflect genuine interest and curiosity. No judgments on the merits of one culture over another should be permitted. Each should be accepted at face value and appreciated for its uniqueness. This sharing creates an atmosphere of mutual respect and openness. You may encourage students to bring in photographs or pictures from magazines depicting the elements of culture they are discussing.

Many options are available to you for varying your use of the *Let's Share* section. We suggest the following options.

1. The first time the *Let's Share* section is used, you may want to lead the discussion with the class as a whole. That way you can establish a tone of mutual respect and appreciation.

2. You may ask students to work in groups of three or four. Assign one student in each group the task of reporting to the class about what the group has discussed.
3. Organize the students into pairs. Assign one student the role of speaker and the other the role of listener. For five minutes, the speaker must discuss his or her culture with regard to the *Let's Share* page. Tell the other student to listen carefully but not to take notes. When the speaker has finished talking, the listener must repeat what he or she has heard. The speaker then says whether the listener has reported the information correctly. The students then change roles. This is an excellent way to increase listening comprehension and to make sure that the listener is, in fact, paying attention.

Model Dialogues

Before students are asked to provide dialogue or to converse, they are provided with model conversations. The conversations should be practiced orally, with appropriate body language and gestures. Here are some guidelines.

1. Have students discuss what body language would be appropriate for each person in the dialogue. (Students may refer to *Gestures and Body Language* in chapter 1.)
2. Once the body language has been established, ask students to act out the model dialogues using appropriate gestures.
3. In more advanced classes, you can ask students if there is other body language that could be used. They can then act out the dialogue using alternative body language. The class can then discuss if the body language changed the meaning of the dialogue.
4. Suggest that students enact the dialogues in different ways:
   a. Have two students enact the dialogue while laughing.
   b. Have two students enact the dialogue very seriously.
   c. Have them enact the dialogue not looking at each other.

Discuss how each approach changes the meaning of the words.

Now You Do It

Once students have completed the cultural sharing, practiced the idioms and phrases, and manipulated the model dialogues, they are ready to prepare responses to half dialogues. This is the next step from sample dialogues, and it leads to free conversations and role-plays. Here are some guidelines for presenting this feature.

1. Have students work in small groups or pairs to complete the half dialogues.
2. Have more advanced students write an original conversation.
3. Once the students have written the dialogues, you can choose among these suggestions.
   a. Ask students to take turns practicing the dialogues.
   b. Ask students to discuss appropriate facial and hand gestures for each person in the dialogue. Then ask two students to act them out, with appropriate gestures, in front of the class.
   c. If several tape recorders are available, ask students in each group to tape their dialogues. Then you can play the tapes so the students can hear how they sound.
   d. You may wish to tape or videotape some of the conversations. Then you can write them on the chalkboard and point out grammatical elements and idiomatic usage. Use the videotape to discuss the facial and hand gestures as well as language elements.
   e. Have students practice the dialogues with the tapes that accompany *Culturally Speaking.*

Role-Play

In *Role-play*, the students are given a situation and must respond spontaneously. Role-plays come closest to natural conversation because the participants in the role-plays do not know in advance what their partner is going to say. Here are some guidelines for using role-plays in class.

1. Have students work in pairs, enacting situations while you circulate, listen to the conversation, and provide assistance when necessary.
2. You might tape several conversations and transcribe them onto the chalkboard; then discuss grammatical forms and appropriate use of idioms.
3. To improve listening comprehension, divide the class into groups. Have two students converse while a third listens and writes down observations.

Analysis   *Analysis* sections are closely related to *Let's Share* sections. As students analyze how people in other countries do or perceive things and make comparisons with their own culture, they arrive at a deeper understanding of themselves and of others. The information provided in these sections becomes the basis for later communication practice.

Quick Customs Quiz   The *Quick Customs Quiz* is a fast-paced exercise in which students read situations and choose the answer they think is the most appropriate way to deal with the situation. Answers at the end of the book reflect how a mainstream North American would respond in a similar situation. The exercise asks students to choose answers as they think a North American would or to choose as they would for their culture. Follow up with a class discussion of the answers.

You may choose to assign the *Quick Customs Quiz* for homework, asking students to come to class prepared to discuss their answers. During in-class discussion, students can make cross-cultural comparisons. [Encourage students to discuss how they feel about dealing with situations in the way the book suggests (in the answer key) a mainstream North American would act.] You may also discuss alternative methods of handling situations.

Idioms, Phrases, and Expressions   Some situations require knowledge of special terminology. Therefore, key idioms, phrases, and expressions—such as those people use when dating, eating out, going to the doctor, making introductions, responding to invitations, and using the telephone—are provided. Students learn the terms in a conversational context, for example through model dialogues; then they use them in a variety of ways, such as making sentences on their own. (You can have students rewrite the sentences, substituting a blank for the expression given. Then you can have students exchange papers and fill in the appropriate expression in the blank spaces.)

What's Going On Here?   In *What's Going On Here?* students read about situations in which there is a cultural misunderstanding. The misunderstandings cause people to become offended, angry, or confused. Students must determine what went wrong and why. Discussion questions follow each description, anecdote, or dialogue to help students determine the cultural problem. The questions are also meant to stimulate discussion about how the problem might have been prevented or to help students come up with other ways to deal with the situation.

Exploring North America   This section encourages a hands-on analysis of North American culture, customs, and attitudes. This is one of the most valuable sections because it forces students to become involved with important issues and actions and requires that they observe, ask questions, and form opinions based on actual experiences and interactions.

These exercises may be used in several ways.

1. Have the students complete the questions either individually or with a partner.

2. To gather information for the *Exploring North America* sections, encourage students to observe and to interview as many individuals as possible rather than concentrating on only one or two people.

3. Have students discuss answers in small groups, for sharing, or in large groups. It's important to discuss both the **what** and the **why** in each section. Note and discuss similarities and differences in students' observations.

4. You may also wish to have your students keep an *Exploring North America* log for weekly individual and class discussions.

5. If your students are unable to interview or observe North Americans directly, you can have your students view videotapes which will illustrate the areas under discussion.

Speaking Out   This section provides thought-provoking information and questions for in-class discussion, encouraging students to analyze and explore situations and issues which provide a deeper insight into North American culture and attitudes.

These exercises may be used in a variety of ways.

1. Have students form small groups to discuss the issues conversationally. You may want the groups to analyze the questions and then to formulate their response for a larger group discussion.

2. Have students meet in large-group discussions to facilitate an understanding of North American attitudes and culture.

3. Ask students to hold discussions which compare and contrast North American attitudes and culture with those of other nationalities.

4. Ask students to do research to gather data documenting issues and information provided through the discussion questions.

5. Suggest that students use the information to create a "Speaking Out Journal" in which students note North American issues and attitudes which they have observed and would like to discuss.

6. Have students use the material from the questions as a basis for in-class debates.

Answers   Answers to the exercises are provided in a separate section at the end of the book. Sometimes cultural elements are elaborated on to provide students with a better understanding of the concepts presented.

Glossary   The glossary at the end of the book provides definitions for the difficult words and idioms used in the text. It also gives their part of speech and uses each item in a sentence so that students may see each word used in an appropriate context.

One

Getting Along with People

Each of us from different cultural backgrounds has a unique way of doing things, analyzing situations, and reacting to circumstances. Our individual way of viewing a situation is called **perception.**

Look at the pictures below. What do you see?

Depending on your perception, you will see either a vase or the profile of two faces in figure *A*. In figure *B*, depending on your perception, you will see either an old woman or a young woman. (See page 177 for the solution to figure *B*.)

Just as our perception of lines in black and white can be changed, so can our perceptions of life. This difference in perceptions makes up cultures.

A

B

To live comfortably in another country, you need to understand its citizens' thinking and expectations. In *Culturally Speaking,* you will experience how people in the United States and Canada think, live, and act. You will also see how they perceive others and interpret actions and behaviors. At the same time, you will compare your own culture, traditions, and ways of responding to situations and share them with your classmates. As you share your knowledge and learn from others, you will not only learn English but also begin to understand life in North America.

1 Introductions

Everyone wants to meet people and make friends. A smile, a friendly look, or an open gesture indicates a person's interest in you. To introduce yourself, approach a person, smile, and say, "Hello, my name is _____." Then shake hands with your friend by firmly taking his or her right hand in yours and pressing it gently but firmly.

Introducing Yourself

Stand up and turn to the person next to you. Put your hand out, shake hands, and introduce yourselves. You may use the dialogue below or similar language. After introducing yourselves, answer the questions that follow.

Hello, my name is _____.

It's nice to meet you. I'm _____.

Discussion questions

After introducing yourselves, discuss these questions with your classmates.

1. Did the person smile when introducing himself or herself?
2. What was the handshake like?
   limp?   too soft and weak?
   strong and firm?   cold?
   too hard?   hot and clammy?
3. Did the handshake last too long?
4. Did the person hold your fingers or slide his or her hand up to your thumb?
5. Were you comfortable shaking hands?
6. Did either of you bow?
7. Where did the other person look when speaking?
8. Where did you look?
9. How far apart did you stand?

All of these things are very important and will be discussed in this chapter. Each gesture, movement, and look sends a message to the other person.

Let's Share

Here is a chart that outlines how North Americans greet each other. Compare these customs with customs in your country. Describe or demonstrate the body language you would use in your country.

What Is the Right Action?	In North America	In Your Country
1. Who makes the introduction?	Either the person who wishes to meet another or a friend who knows the other person makes the introduction.	
2. Who should be introduced to whom?	A younger person should be introduced to an older person, a subordinate to a superior.	
3. What should you say?	"Hello, my name is _____." "Mary Smith, I'd like you to meet my friend, John Jones." "Dr. Raman, this is my associate, Professor Allen." "Mrs. Buckett, I'd like to introduce my daughter, Jennifer."	
4. May a man introduce himself to a woman? May a woman introduce herself to a man?	Yes; yes.	
5. What body language (facial expressions, gestures) should a person use?	Smile, face the person, and look attentively at the person's eyes.	
6. What tone of voice should you use?	Use a quiet but friendly tone.	

Box continued on the following page

Box continued from the preceding page

What Is the Right Action?	In North America	In Your Country
7. Does a person shake hands when meeting someone? How should you shake hands?	Men and women usually shake hands firmly but gently.	
8. Do people embrace or kiss people of the same sex upon meeting? Do you kiss or hug children when they are introduced?	No, unless the people are very close friends. Men kiss each other if they are relatives or very close friends. Not usually.	

Now You Do It   Now that we have discussed introductions, it's time for you to do it.

Complete and then practice the following conversation, which is appropriate at work, in school, in your neighborhood, or in any place where the same people usually see each other and would recognize you as being new.

STRANGER: Hi. You're new here, aren't you?

YOU: _____.

STRANGER: My name is Barbara Levinson.

YOU: Will you say that again, please?

STRANGER: Yes, my name is Barbara Levinson. What is your name?

YOU: _____.

STRANGER: How do you spell that?

YOU: _____.

STRANGER: I'm really glad to meet you.

YOU: _____.

As you can see from this dialogue, it is perfectly acceptable to ask someone to speak more slowly or to repeat what he or she has said. The other person will be pleased that you want to understand and are willing to ask questions.

4

2 Small Talk

After the introduction, people usually talk about topics of general interest, such as the weather, local events, work, or school. This is called **small talk.** These topics can be discussed easily without knowing the other person well. They are very good conversation starters.

Sometimes using small talk is a way to meet someone or to start a conversation. Here are some examples.

In a classroom:

YOU: Hello, aren't you in my English class?

OTHER PERSON: Yes, I thought I'd seen you there before.

YOU: Did you finish the essay?

OTHER PERSON: No, I had trouble organizing my thoughts.

At a dance:

YOU: Excuse me. Do you know when the band's going to start playing?

OTHER PERSON: I'm not sure — maybe about nine-thirty.

YOU: Do you know if they've recorded any songs yet? I don't think I've ever heard of them before.

OTHER PERSON: I don't think so, but they're supposed to be really good.

Model Dialogues

Here are some examples of small talk.

1. PERSON A: Hi!

   PERSON B: Hello.

   A: It's a nice day, isn't it?

   B: Yes, and the weather is going to be warm all week. . . .

2. A: Did you see the paper this morning?

   B: No, why?

   A: There was a terrible accident on the road into town!

   B: Really? What happened? . . .

3. A: Did you see the football game on TV last night?

   B: No, who was playing?

   A: The Green Bay Packers and the Detroit Lions.

   B: What was the score? . . .

4. A: When is it going to stop snowing?

   B: On TV they predicted snow until evening.

   A: Oh no, really?

   B: Yes, and another storm is moving in! . . .

Here is an example of an introduction followed by small talk.

5. ROBERT: Mr. Caldwell, I'd like you to meet my mother.

   MR. CALDWELL: Mrs. Rienzo, I'm pleased to meet you.

   MRS. RIENZO: Robert enjoys your class very much.

   MR. CALDWELL: Thank you. I enjoy having him in class.

   MRS. RIENZO: It was very nice meeting you.

   MR. CALDWELL: Same here. Good-bye.

Introductions among young people or casual acquaintances are less formal. For example, an eight- or nine-year-old child would probably say, "Mom, this is my friend Peter." It is important to know that North Americans, especially men, do not embrace unless they are very good friends who have not seen each other for a long time.

Here are some examples of introductions.

Introducing two friends:

TIM: John, I'd like you to meet my friend, Joan Sullivan. Joan, this is John Tracy.

JOAN: (*shaking hands with John*) It's nice to meet you.

Introducing your friend to your mother:

TIM: Phyllis, I'd like you to meet my mother, Mrs. Abrams. Mom, this is Phyllis Akerly.

PHYLLIS: I'm glad to meet you, Mrs. Abrams.

MRS. ABRAMS: I'm happy to meet you, too. Tim has talked so much about you.

Here are some more sample introductions. Notice that the person making the introduction provides a little information about the person he or she is introducing. This often helps to start a conversation between the people who are being introduced.

1. TOM: Mr. O'Malley, I'd like you to meet my friend Maria Carlos. She's an exchange student from Spain, and she's majoring in computer science.

   MR. O'MALLEY: I'm glad to meet you. I hope you've been able to get the courses you want. Computer science is such a popular major.

   MARIA: Yes, thank you, I have. Fortunately, there are a lot of courses to choose from.

   MR. O'MALLEY: That's good.

   MARIA: Well, I have to go to class now. I certainly enjoyed meeting you.

   MR. O'MALLEY: I hope we'll meet again. Good-bye.

   MARIA: Good-bye.

2. HEATHER: Hello, I'm Heather Allen.

   SUSAN: Hi, I'm Susan Miselli. It's nice to meet you.

   HEATHER: Same here. Do you know Steven Johnson? He and I sell computers.

   SUSAN: No. (*shakes hands*) How do you do? That sounds like interesting work.

   STEVEN: Yes, it is. I've been working for Computer Installations for four years in the Hardware Division.

SUSAN: Do you sell personal or business computers?

STEVEN: Mostly personal. You wouldn't believe how much the industry has changed in the last year!

SUSAN: What's happened? . . .

(A third person, Molly, joins Heather and Susan. Steven has gone to talk with another friend.)

MOLLY: Hello, Heather.

HEATHER: Hi, Molly.

MOLLY: How are you?

HEATHER: Fine. Do you know Susan?

MOLLY: No, I don't.

HEATHER: Molly, this is Susan Miselli. Susan, this is Molly Blair.

SUSAN: Pleased to meet you.

MOLLY: Same here.

HEAHTER: Susan is a singer.

MOLLY: How interesting! Where do you sing?

SUSAN: Well, I'm studying music right now, but I hope someday to sing at the Metropolitan Opera House.

MOLLY: That's wonderful! I hope you get that opportunity.

SUSAN: Thank you. What do you do?

MOLLY: I'm an electrical engineer. I work at the same company as Heather.

What might Susan say to continue the conversation?

Conversation Topics

Some good things to talk about with your new friend include the following:

1. The country you or the other person is from (What is it like? How does it compare to the United States or Canada?)
2. What the other person is studying or has studied in school (What are you studying in school? What is your favorite subject? What do you want to do after you graduate?)
3. The work that the other person does (What kind of work do you do? Do you like it? What do you enjoy about it? How did you decide to go into teaching, programming, painting, electronics, etc?)
4. North America (What do you like about the United States/Canada? What interesting things have happened since you came here? How does this compare to your country?)
5. Your family
6. Current events
7. The weather

Topics may vary according to the situation, the people you are with and the type of function you are attending. There are, however, some subjects that you should not talk about, especially with someone you don't know well. These include the following:

1. How much money you have or make
2. How much someone paid for something
3. Sexual subjects

4. Class, status or racial issues
5. A person's age
6. A person's weight

    These are very sensitive subjects because North Americans take them very personally. Even though you do not mean to offend them, they may be upset if you ask questions about these subjects.

Let's Share   To compare acceptable and unacceptable topics of conversation in the United States and Canada with those from your country, fill in this chart. When you have finished, share this information with your fellow class members.

                                                                       (name of your country)

Acceptable Topics of Conversation	*Unacceptable Topics of Conversation*
1. _____	1. _____
2. _____	2. _____
3. _____	3. _____
4. _____	4. _____
5. _____	5. _____

Look at these topics carefully. What are the differences between North American topics and topics from your country? What does this tell you about the people of both countries.

    Here are some more pointers about conversation. When you are talking with your friend, listen carefully and let the conversation continue. Don't just ask one question after another or answer your friend's questions with one-word answers. In North America, as in most places, people feel uneasy if you ask a lot of questions or answer in one-word replies. They will think that you are being "pushy" or that you are uninterested in what they have to say. Be prepared to tell about yourself and your interests as well as to ask about the other person. In this way, both you and your listener can share information and learn about each other. You should also be aware that North Americans are uncomfortable with silence in conversation and will always try to think of something to say to fill the gap. You, however, may feel very comfortable with silence.

3   Distance and Space Requirements

Space Requirements   People from different cultures have different space requirements. For example, Latin Americans and Middle Easterners stand closer when they talk than do North Americans or Asians.

    In the United States and Canada, people need to have greater distances between them physically than do people in many other cultures. Although North Americans are often more affectionate and more likely to touch people they know, they have a great need for privacy, especially in the presence of strangers. For example, when North

Americans enter a bus, a doctor's office, or a waiting room, they sit at least one chair away from the nearest person, if possible. Conversation distance with superiors or with those they don't know well is about three to four feet.* However, intimate conversations may be held as close as one-and-a-half feet apart. Because North Americans feel uncomfortable if someone stands closer, they will instinctively move away. Should this happen, don't be offended. Your listener is merely stepping back to his or her normal conversational distance.

Analysis

Countries do not have the same "rules" about how close to each other people should sit or stand. Fill in the chart below for your country. The first situation has been filled in for North America. When you have completed the chart, compare your answers with those on page 177, which are the answers an American or Canadian would give.

Situation	Distance People Sit or Stand From Each Other	Type of Body Language People Use
1. Riding on a bus with people you don't know	People try to sit at least one seat from another person and avoid touching. They stand as far apart as possible.	Looking away or out the window, reading, crossing arms, clutching packages
2. Waiting in a doctor's office		
3. Waiting in line		
4. Eating lunch in a restaurant or café		
5. Talking to your boss or teacher		
6. Talking to friends in a group		
7. Talking to a stranger		
8. Talking to a child		

*Note: 12 inches = 1 foot; 1 inch = 2.54 centimeters.

Answer these questions about your own country to come up with a set of rules about distance in your culture. Then demonstrate the appropriate distance.

1. You wish to carry on a conversation with a person you don't know well. How far apart should you stand from this person? _____

2. You wish to talk intimately with someone you know well. How far apart should you be? _____

3. You are talking to a supervisor or an elder (your employer, a teacher, a clergyman, a government official). How far away should you stand? _____

4. When you enter a bus, a restaurant, a doctor's office, or any waiting room, how close should you sit to the nearest person? _____

4 Hand Gestures

Even before people begin to talk, you can tell a great deal about them by observing their gestures. Gestures can tell about a person's attitudes, feelings, and interests.

Analysis Gestures may have more than one meaning. In fact, they may mean something totally different from one culture to the next. Look at the photograph below and at the one on page 11.

Each played an important role in understanding and misunderstanding in history. The first was taken when Soviet leader Brezhnev visited with U.S. President Nixon. When Americans saw this photograph they became angry because clasped hands are a sign of victory in the United States. Americans interpreted this picture to mean that Brezhnev thought he had won in his talks with the U.S. president. But in Russia clasped hands means friendship!

The next photograph was taken when the American ship *Pueblo* was captured by North Korea in 1968. The men confessed to crimes, and then this picture was taken. When the Americans saw the photograph, they knew the men had lied to their confessors. How did they know?

If you look carefully, you will notice that three of the men are pointing their middle finger. Displaying this finger is a great insult in the United States.

Let's Share   As we have seen, gestures can have more than one meaning. In fact, they can mean something totally different from country to country. Look at the photographs on the following pages and write below what they mean in your country. If they do not have a special meaning in your country, present a different gesture from your country and explain what it means.

1.

In North America this gesture means approval.

In _____ this gesture means _____.

2.

In North America this gesture means good, acceptable, or okay.

In _____ this gesture means _____.

3.

In North America this gesture means to stop.

In _____ this gesture means _____.

4.

In North America this gesture means good luck.

In _____ this gesture means _____.

5.

In North America this gesture means victory.

In _____ this gesture means _____.

6.

In North America this gesture means "come here."

In _____ this gesture means _____.

7.

In North America this gesture means success.

In _____ this gesture means _____.

8.

In North America this gesture means good-bye.

In _____ this gesture means _____.

9.

In North America this gesture means "it's no good," or failure.

In _____ this gesture means _____.

10.

In North America this gesture means "give it to me."

In _____ this gesture means _____.

11.

In North America this gesture means "I don't know."

In _____ this gesture means _____.

12.

In North America this gesture means you want someone to give you a ride.

In _____ this gesture means _____.

13.

In North America this gesture shows anger and a desire to hit someone.

In _____ this gesture shows _____.

14.

In North America this gesture means you want to interrupt to say something.

In _____ this gesture means _____.

Using Idioms

Below are examples of idioms related to hand gestures. They are used in context. Try to use the context to guess the meaning of the idioms.

1. The teacher looked angrily at Steven and told him *to hand it over.* He reluctantly gave her the note he had been trying to pass to Jennifer.
2. Jane's desk is so tidy she has everything she needs right *at her fingertips.*
3. Peter and Susan must be in love. Whenever I see them they are walking *hand in hand.*
4. Aaron wants me to lie about the accident, but I don't want *to stick my neck out* for him. Why should I lie for him?
5. Mrs. Dexter's class is so boring. We just sit there and *twiddle our thumbs.*
6. Ever since Mary found out that David had gone out with another girl, she's been *giving him the cold shoulder.* I don't blame her. I wouldn't talk to him either.
7. I'm going over to Mike's tomorrow *to give him a hand* moving. He has so much stuff he can't possibly do it all by himself.
8. I've never learned how to fish, so I thought I'd *try my hand at* it. Do you want to come with me?
9. Al went looking for a new CD player all day yesterday, but he came home *empty handed.* He was so disappointed. I guess he'll have to look again next week.
10. Mary asked William to go to the dance with her next week. I guess she doesn't know he *has two left feet.* I hope she doesn't wear new shoes!
11. A simple *rule of thumb* is to give an honest answer to any question. That kind of common-sense approach will save you a lot of trouble later on.
12. I hate to see Alison and Tom together. She has him *wrapped around her little finger.* It makes me sick to see him do every little thing she wants.

13. At the car accident this big guy *gave* the other driver *the finger*. It made me so mad to see him use a disgusting, nasty gesture, especially since the accident was his fault!
14. People are not allowed to hitchhike on the New York State Thruway, but I saw two people *thumbing rides* there yesterday.
15. I have to *hand it* to him. He wasn't good in calculus, but he studied every day and got an *A* in the course. He deserves to be complimented.
16. That jerk! He told Donald that he loved his new suit. Then he asked, "Where did you get it—at the new discount store?" What a *backhanded compliment*!
17. I dropped three things today. Boy, do I have *butterfingers*!

Matching: Gesture Idioms

The English language is rich in idioms. In the left-hand column are some commonly used idioms that involve gestures. Try to match each idiom with its correct meaning from the right-hand column. Check your answers on page 178.

Part 1

_I_ 1. To give someone a hand

___ 2. To try your hand at something

_G_ 3. To have butterfingers

___ 4. To hand it over

_E_ 5. To be hand in hand

___ 6. To give a backhanded compliment

_A_ 7. To twiddle your thumbs

___ 8. To finger something or someone

_F_ 9. To hand it to someone

A. To be bored; to have nothing to do
B. To make an unflattering remark
C. To say someone is right
D. To attempt something new
E. To hold hands
F. To give someone something
G. To be clumsy
H. To steal or to tell on someone
I. To help someone

Part 2

_J_ 10. To give someone the finger

_L_ 11. To thumb a ride

___ 12. To be at your finger tips

_K_ 13. To give someone the cold shoulder

_N_ 14. To be empty-handed

J. To insult someone
K. To ignore someone
L. To hitchhike
M. To be clumsy
N. To have nothing
O. To have things handy
P. To be under someone's control or influence
Q. To take a chance
R. To use common sense

16

_____M___ 15. To have two left feet

_____P___ 16. To be wrapped around some-
one's little finger

_____ 17. To stick your neck out

_____ 18. To follow a rule of thumb

Role-play   Below are three situations to act out in class.

1. You are in a crowded room, and you see someone you know come in. You can't shout, but you want to catch the person's eye and find out how he or she did on a test.
2. You are standing in line at a buffet, and your friend is four people ahead of you. He's new to the United States and has never eaten American food before. As he reaches for each item, he looks at you. Using facial gestures, demonstrate which foods are good and which aren't. Be sure to distinguish between those foods you really like, those that are just all right, and those you dislike.
3. You have laryngitis and your friend is leaving to take an exam. Using your hands, wish your friend good luck, also, wish her an excellent grade, and then say good-bye.

Gestures We Use with Others   Look at the gestures pictured below. Do you have the same or similar gestures in your country? When do you use them? Do you use them in the same circumstances that North Americans do? Discuss them with your classmates.

1. Kissing on the cheek: to greet and say good-bye to relatives and good friends

2. Having hands raised and touching: to show shared victory

3. Patting someone on the back: to congratulate someone

4. Putting an arm around someone: to get closer to someone; to try to comfort someone to show friendship

5. Shaking hands with someone: to meet and say good-bye to someone in a formal way

6. Putting your index finger across your throat (as if it were a knife): to show that you have made a terrible mistake and that someone is going to be so angry they'd like to kill you

7. Hugging someone: to show warm affection between relatives and friends

Acting Out a Dialogue

Act out these situations with a partner. Use gestures as you talk with and respond to the other person.

Situation 1:

Person 1: (*comes running off the tennis court after having won the match*)

Person 2: (*runs over to congratulate him*)

Person 3: (*a team member who is also part of the winning team comes over*) Person 1 and person 3 congratulate each other.

Situation 2:

John is your roommate. You and he have become very good friends. He gets off the telephone and tells you that his scholarship has been denied and he has to leave school.

Situation 3:

You and a friend are in your room. You have been playing your roommate's CD player. He doesn't like you to use it when he isn't there, but you are being very careful. Unfortunately, something happens and the CD gets stuck in the player and you can't get it out. You can hear your roommate coming. As you act out the scene, signal to your friend that your roommate is going to kill you.

Situation 4:

You are sitting in your classroom waiting to hear your grade on the last test. It's very important that you pass the test because you have a failing grade so far. Your friend is in the hall signaling to you. He wants to know how you did. At first, you don't know. Then the teacher says you received an *A*. You signal to your friend that you did well.

5 Facial Gestures

Let's Share

Look at these pictures of facial gestures. After reading the explanations, fill in the blanks with information about how the gestures are used in your country or in a classmate's country. Leave blank any that are not used in your country.

1.

In North America this gesture is used by children to show dislike or contempt.

In _____ this gesture means _____.

2.

In North America this gesture means surprise and can show some snobbishness.

In _____ this gesture means _____.

3.

In North America this gesture means dismay or some mild disagreement.

In _____ this gesture means _____.

4.

In North America this gesture shows unhappiness.

In _____ this gesture shows _____.

5.

In North America this gesture shows displeasure.

In _____ this gesture shows _____.

6.

In North America this gesture shows anger.

In _____ this gesture shows _____.

7.

In North America this gesture shows disbelief.

In _____ this gesture shows _____.

8.

In North America this gesture shows that you won a game or competition, or that you want to stand up to or challenge someone.

In _____ this gesture shows _____.

9.

In North America this gesture shows insincerity.

In _____ this gesture shows _____.

10.

In North America this gesture shows boredom.

In _____ this gesture shows _____.

11.

In North America this gesture means "no."

In _____ this gesture means _____.

12.

In North America this gesture means "yes."

In _____ this gesture means _____.

6 Summary

By comparing the customs and cultures of people from other countries, we can learn how others view the world and why they think the way they do. By understanding others, we not only can form deeper friendships with others but can also learn more about ourselves and our own culture. Think carefully about your answers to these questions.

1. In what significant ways do the gestures and body language used in your country differ from those used in North America?
2. In what ways do the gestures and body language used in your country resemble those used in North America?
3. How are the customs for making conversation in North America different from those in your country?
4. Which customs for making conversation in North America are the same as in your country?
5. What other country did you learn about from your classmates? What was especially interesting to you about that country?
6. Which of the North American customs that you have studied do you find difficult to deal with? Why?
7. Which North American customs seem the most natural to you? Why?

Now You Do It   Choose an identity you would like as your own—for example, that of a famous movie star, a world leader, an ambassador, a teacher, or a musician. Write your new name and occupation on a sheet of paper. Below this, write your real name. Give this paper to the teacher.

Now pretend that you and your classmates are at a party at a friend's house. Using your new name, introduce yourself to two other people and learn their names and occupations. Then introduce them to each other. When you introduce them, be sure to tell each what the other person does so that they can make small talk.

Minisimulation

Now that you know about small talk and have read the example, you are ready for the *Mini-simulation*. You have 15 minutes to accomplish this. Follow the same directions under the **Now You Do It** section. Use the name and profession you wrote down and gave to your teacher to make your introductions. At social functions where there are many people, the guests usually stand and talk briefly to a lot of people. If possible, move the furniture in your room to one side, or gather in the front of the room.

Discussion questions

At the end of the "party," discuss the following questions.

1. Were you able to meet two or more people? How many did you meet?
2. Introduce to the class one of the people you met. Give his or her name and occupation.
3. Did making introductions become easier for you? Why?
4. What kind of small talk did you make? Did you talk about professions? the weather? the news?
5. Did you have any problems? What were they?

A. Read the dialogue below. See if you can guess what the problem was. Then, with your classmates, answer the questions that follow.

MARY ANN: Hello my name is Mary Ann.

PAULA: Hi, I'm Paula.

MARY ANN: I really like your dress. How much did it cost?

PAULA: Well, I uh, I don't remember for sure.

MARY ANN: Your shoes are nice too. They look expensive. How much did they cost? Did you get them on sale?

PAULA: I have to be going now. I'll see you later.

Discussion questions

1. Why didn't Mary Ann tell Paula how much her dress and shoes cost?
2. What do you think Paula's body language was when Mary Ann asked her these questions?
3. Why did Paula leave so quickly after meeting Mary Ann?
4. What could Mary Ann have talked about instead?
5. Do you think Paula really did remember how much her dress and shoes cost and was telling Mary Ann a *white lie*? (A white lie is an untruth that doesn't hurt anyone.)

B. Read the story below, and try to figure out what is going on. Then, with your classmates, answer the questions.

Kristin has been invited to an American home for a party. She has been in the United States for only a week, and she is happy that her classmate has invited her over.

When Kristin arrives at the party, there are very few people there. As she takes her coat off, she notices her American host talking to a tall man in a brown sweater. As they speak, Kristin sees her host take one step and then another backward. The man in the brown sweater then takes two steps forward.

Kristin notices that her American host is smiling with her mouth closed; Kristin senses that something is wrong. Fascinated, she watches them. Then she sees the host step back again; the tall man in the brown sweater, smiling all the time, takes two steps forward again. Can this be some kind of dance?

Finally, the host catches Kristin's eye, and, smiling at the man in the brown sweater, says, "Excuse me. I must greet my new guest."

When the host comes over to welcome Kristin, she says, "You came just in time. I'm so glad to see you!"

Discussion questions

1. What do you think was the problem?
2. Why was the hostess glad to see Kristin?
3. Do you think the man in the brown sweater knew that something was wrong?
4. Why do you think the hostess kept taking steps backward?
5. Why do you think the man in the brown sweater kept taking steps forward?

C. Read the following situation, and think about what is happening. Then, with your classmates, answer the questions.

Jennifer had a doctor's appointment at 3:00 P.M. The waiting room was empty, and she took a seat next to the magazine table. She picked up one of the magazines and began to read. After her busy morning, it was pleasant to have a quiet environment in which to read.

In a few minutes another patient arrived with two young children. She took the chair next to Jennifer and told her children to find something to read. One of the boys gave his mother a storybook and asked her to read it. When she pulled the child up onto her lap, his foot accidentally kicked Jennifer. The mother apologized and began to read the story to him.

Jennifer looked around at the empty waiting room. Then she got up from her seat and moved to the other side of the room, where there were four empty seats.

Discussion questions

1. Where did Jennifer sit when she came into the waiting room?
2. Was there anyone else in the waiting room when she arrived?
3. Where did the next patient sit when she came into the room? Who was with her?
4. Why do you think she sat there?
5. Why did Jennifer get up and move to the other side of the room?

D. Read about John's experience at a neighbor's party. Then discuss the questions below with your classmates.

John has been invited to a party at a neighbor's house. When he arrives, there are manypeople standing, drinking, eating, and talking. Everyone is holding a glass in one hand and eating potato chips, fruit, cheese and crackers, and hot hors d'oeuvres. They all seem happy, talking and laughing. As he looks around the room, he sees that there are many chairs but that no one is sitting down.

Suddenly, he feels a slap on his back and hears someone say, "Hi, neighbor!" He becomes uncomfortable, but when he turns around, he sees another neighbor. They talk for a few minutes, and then his neighbor says, "Oh excuse me. I see a friend of mine on the other side of the room." Then he leaves. John wonders why he left so quickly. They were just starting to have an interesting conversation. John decides to ask the host if he can give him a hand.

Discussion questions

1. Why is everyone standing when there are empty chairs?
2. How do you think John felt when he got slapped on the back?
3. Why did the neighbor leave after talking to John for only a few minutes? Is this common at this type of party?

Exploring North America

In this exercise you will have an opportunity to watch people and analyze their use of gestures.

A. Gestures are an important part of communication. Observe North Americans and determine the gestures they use; then observe how their use of gestures varies depending on the situation.

1. Compare the types, amount, and size of gestures a person uses when making a formal speech to an audience with those he or she uses when having a casual conversation with a friend.
2. Compare the types, amount, and size of gestures an adult uses when speaking to a child with those he or she uses when speaking to another adult.
3. Compare the gestures a person who is expressing anger uses with those a person who is speaking calmly uses.

B. If possible, either through observing other students or by analyzing television news programs, note the differences in the use of gestures by North Americans from different ethnic groups and from different regions of the country. What differences in types, amount, and size of gestures do you see?

C. Watch two people having a conversation. Observe their gestures and distance from each other. Then answer these questions.

1. Is the conversation a formal (business) conversation or an informal conversation? How do you know?
2. Looking at their speaking distance, eye contact, and gestures, can you tell what the relationship between the speakers is? How do you know?
3. What else can you observe about the speakers?

D. Ask North American students where they go to meet people and what they talk about to begin conversations.

E. Ask your American or Canadian friends what characteristics they look for in a friend and what they think you should do to maintain a friendship.

Speaking Out

Be prepared to discuss the issues presented.

A. For the most part, North Americans are friendly people. When they first meet you, they will try to make you feel welcome by inviting you to their homes or by offering to take you places. They will call you on the telephone often and will be concerned that you are comfortable and have everything you need. However, after some time, your North American friends may not call as often and, if you do not return their friendliness and invitations, they will stop visiting and calling you.

1. Do you think that North Americans are too friendly at first? Why? How can you tell if they are sincere in their offers of friendship?
2. Why do you think North Americans are not as friendly after you get established in your new home? What does this tell you about their view of friendship?
3. What do you need to do to maintain friendships with your North American friends?

B. Americans and Canadians, for the most part, are careful about touching children or people of the same sex. Men do not touch other men except when shaking hands unless they are related. Often, grown sons will not hug or kiss their fathers but will shake hands on meeting or parting. Adults never touch children unless they are related to them. Teachers seldom touch children at school for any reason because they fear someone will think they are molesting them.

1. Ask a North American friend why he or she thinks these statements are true. Ask your friend his or her opinion of how North Americans view touching.
2. What do you think about the North American attitude toward touching people of the same sex or children? Why? How do people from your culture view touching?

Two

Attending School

slouching
upright

Cultures have developed particular styles of teaching. Therefore, moving from one country to another to study may present some surprises for students.

In some cultures, it is rude for students to ask their teachers questions. Questioning the teacher is like saying the teacher has not done a good job explaining the subject. In some cultures, students learn through rote memorization and believe that what the teacher says is always the truth. In other cultures, students are taught to think for themselves. The role of the teacher is to stimulate their thinking, to get them to ask questions, to challenge—even to argue with—the teacher, and to come to their own conclusions. In some parts of the world, grades depend on the status of your family and not on your ability in a subject.

Studies indicate that people like to learn differently. Some people learn better by listening, while others need to see the information. Your answers to the questions below may give you some idea of how you prefer to learn. When you have answered them, compare your answers with those of other people in your class.

1. I prefer to learn by listening to the teacher lecture. (Yes or no)
2. I prefer to learn by reading and studying my texts. (Yes or no)
3. I prefer to learn by studying or working with other people. (Yes or no)
4. I prefer to study by myself. (Yes or no)
5. I like to ask the teacher questions. (Yes or no)
6. When I study for a test, I
   a. read my notes.
   b. say my notes aloud.
   c. rewrite my notes.
7. I remember best
   a. smells.
   b. tastes.
   c. sounds.
   d. sights.
   e. touches.
8. If I received as a gift a machine with many buttons on it, I would
   a. read the directions first.
   b. play with the buttons first.
   c. ask someone to show me how it works
9. I like to
   a. memorize facts.
   b. think about ideas.
10. This is how people are taught in my culture. (Explain.)

In this chapter, we will share information about attending school in our own countries and learn some of the customs for being successful in North American schools.

1 Learning About North American Schools

Before we discuss schools in North America, take a few minutes to discuss schools in your country. Meet in a group with three or four other students, and share information about schools you have attended in your country. Use these questions as a guide for your discussion.

1. What do students wear to school?
2. How do students get to school?
3. How do students know which class to go to? Are there different classes, or does everyone study in one room?
4. How do students greet the teacher? What do they say? What body language do they use? Do they stand?
5. How does the teacher greet the students?
6. Do students bring gifts to the teacher? If so, when? What do they bring?
7. How do students address the teacher: Mr., Ms., Mrs., Dr., Professor, Teacher, or by his or her first name?

8. When does the school year begin? How long does it last? How long is the school day?
9. Who decides what a student will study?
10. Who decides which students will attend college and what they will study? Why?

As you work through this chapter, compare the customs in your country with those in the United States and Canada.

Quick Customs Quiz

Below are situations in which you might find yourself in the United States or Canada. Read each situation, decide what is appropriate, and choose the answer that best fits the circumstances. Draw a circle around the letter in front of your answer. Check your answers against those on page 178, which are the answers an American or a Canadian would probably give. (There is more than one possible answer for some of the items.)

1. Your teacher, Mrs. Bills, is walking past you in the hallway, and you wish to catch her attention and say hello. What should you do?

   a. Say, "Hello, Teacher."
   b. Wave your hand.
   c. Smile and say, "Hello, Mrs. Bills."

2. You have not done well on a paper, and your professor has called you into his office to speak to you about your poor grade. When he speaks to you, what should you do?

   a. Look directly into his eyes.
   b. Look down at the floor.
   c. Look up at the ceiling.
   d. Focus your eyes on a distant object.

3. Your math professor has been explaining a problem in class. You understand the first half of the explanation, but you do not understand the rest of the problem. What should you do?

   a. Raise your hand and tell the professor that you don't understand. Ask her to explain the problem again.
   b. Wait until after class and speak to the professor.
   c. After class, ask a friend to explain the problem to you.
   d. Do not ask anyone because this is very embarrassing.
   e. Forget about the problem. You probably will not need to know it anyway.

4. You have an appointment to see your adviser at 10:30 Tuesday morning. On Monday, you develop a fever of 102 degrees Fahrenheit and are clearly too sick to keep your appointment. What should you do?

   a. Call your adviser immediately and cancel the appointment.
   b. Nothing.
   c. Go even though you are very sick. It would be rude not to go.
   d. Ask a friend or roommate to keep the appointment for you.
   e. Write your adviser a note.

5. You are in college and find that you are not doing well in a course. You believe that you are not doing well because you have taken too many courses and are not able to complete all the required assignments. What should you do?

   a. Stop going to class because you don't have time to do the work.
   b. Continue the courses and get your friends to finish your assignments.
   c. See your adviser and ask if you can drop the course.
   d. Speak to the instructor and ask for a grade of "incomplete" so that you can finish the course work during the next semester.

6. You have been doing well in all your classes except social studies. You have the feeling that the teacher doesn't like you. What should you do?

   a. Stop going to class.
   b. Go to class only to take tests.
   c. Speak to your guidance counselor.
   d. Do the best you can under the circumstances.
   e. Speak to the teacher.

7. Your teacher has explained that he determines your grade as follows:

Quizzes	10%
Tests	40%
Reports	30%
Class participation	20%

   You do not like to answer or ask questions in class. What should you do?

   a. Ask to speak to the teacher and explain your shyness.
   b. Tell the teacher you don't think it's fair to put so much emphasis on class participation.
   c. Nothing.

8. While you are taking an examination, you see someone leaning over to copy your paper. What should you do?

   a. Move your paper closer so that he can see.
   b. Tell your professor.
   c. Cover your paper so the other person can't see it.
   d. Tell the other person in a loud voice to stop cheating.

9. You have just received a test paper back from your teacher. She has marked as wrong an answer that you believe to be right because there is another way to interpret the question. What should you do?

   a. Nothing. The teacher should never be questioned.
   b. Raise your hand and ask why your interpretation is wrong.
   c. Speak to the teacher after class.
   d. Complain to the principal or to your parents.

10. You are in history class and the teacher asks for a definition of *free enterprise*. You know the answer. What should you do?

    a. Raise your hand and wait to be called on.
    b. Do not answer the question. That would be showing off.
    c. Wait for the eldest and most respected member of the class to answer.

11. Your teacher has just announced a big test for next Friday. That day is a very holy day in your religion, and you intend to say home to celebrate it. What should you do?

    a. Raise your hand and, when recognized, tell the teacher that Friday is a religious holiday and you won't be in school. Ask the teacher to change the test date.
    b. Come to school and take the test.
    c. Be absent and miss the test.
    d. Go up to the teacher after class and explain the situation.

Discussion questions

After you have completed the *Quick Customs Quiz*, discuss these questions with your classmates.

1. Choose one of the quiz questions and tell how the answer would be different in your culture.
2. Which of these questions is the most difficult for you to do or to understand? Why?
3. Are teachers perceived differently in your culture? How? What is the role of the teacher in your country?

Role-Play   Choose two or three of the situations in the *Quick Customs Quiz* which would be difficult for you to do, and role-play them with a partner.

2 Rules for Attending School

These are the rules for attending school in North America. Indicate whether they are also true in your country by putting a check mark (✔) in the column on the right.

Rule	*Also True in Your Country*
Kindergarten through high school 1. Always refer to a teacher by title and last name: Dr. Walker, Mr. Fields, Mrs. Ramírez, Professor McGuinness. (Never call a teacher "Teacher.")	
2. Arrive in class on time or a little early.	
3. Raise your hand when you want to ask a question.	
4. You may speak to the teacher from your desk while you are seated.	
5. When you are absent, you must make up the work you have missed. Ask the teacher or a classmate for the work.	
6. If you expect to be away from school because of an emergency, tell your teacher in advance, if possible, and ask for the work you will miss.	

Box continued on the following page

Rule	Also True in Your Country
7. All assignments you hand in must be your own work.	
8. Never cheat on a test. (Never look at or copy another student's paper when you are taking a test.)	
9. If you are having difficulty with a class, schedule an appointment to see the teacher for help. The teacher will be glad to help you.	
10. Bring a note from your parent or guardian explaining any absences or tardiness.	
11. You may miss school because of personal illness, a death in the family, or a religious holiday. It is illegal to stay home from school for any other reason.	
12. You may raise your hand to answer a question when a teacher does not name a particular student to answer it.	
College 1. If you receive a failing grade in a course, you will usually need to repeat the course.	
2. You must work hard in your courses.	
3. You must give permission to have your work discussed with your parents.	
4. After taking the required courses in your major, you may select your other courses.	
5. Teachers must consider all students equal in the classroom and must judge them only by the quality of their work.	

Box continued on the following page

Rule	Also True in Your Country
6. You must be entirely responsible for your progress in a course. You must seek help, either with the professor in a lab, if you need help with the work.	
7. Colleges must accept and consider applications from any student who applies.	

After you have completed this assignment, be prepared to discuss your responses with your classmates. Consider how you would feel in a North American class and why. Choose items on the list that you would have the most difficulty accepting. Explain why these would be hard for you. Also be prepared to explain which items refer to things you would do differently in your country and what the rules are for correct school conduct in your country.

Let's Share By comparing the customs and cultures of people from other countries and the way they educate their children, we can gain insights into how they view the world and why they think the way they do. By understanding others, we can also learn more about ourselves. Discuss these questions with your classmates after you have carefully thought about your answers.

1. What are the most important ways in which school in your country differs from school in the United States or Canada?
2. In what significant ways are school in your country and school in the United States or Canada alike?
3. How are students' attitudes toward teachers and school in North America different?
4. What would happen in your country if students acted the way North American students do?
5. Grades are often calculated differently, not only in different countries, but also in the same country. Generally, in the United States and Canada, teachers consider the following areas when computing grades:

   Tests: formal examinations
   Quizzes: short tests, sometimes given to students without telling them in advance
   Homework: work that the students are expected to do individually at home
   Class participation: active involvement in the class, shown by asking and answering questions
   Research paper: a written report that requires finding information in the library
   Attendance: going to class every time it meets
   Promptness: coming to class at exactly the time the class is scheduled to begin and handing in work when it is due
   Attitude: showing interest in the class and respect for the teacher, the subject, and the other students; also, waiting your turn to speak, not interrupting, raising your hand to ask a question
   Are these areas also important in your country? Which ones are not important?

6. Schools in the United States and Canada use their own grading system. However, most grades are either letter grades (*A, B, C, D, F*) or number grades. (In some schools the letter or number grade may vary by one or two points.)

Letter Grade	Number Equivalent	Meaning	
A	90–100	Excellent	
B	80–89	Good	
C	70–79	Average	Passing
D	60–69	Poor	
F	0–59	Failing	

Some schools add a plus or a minus to a grade (for example, *B+, A−*) to indicate that work in a course was a little above or a little below the grade given. What grading system is used in your country? How does it compare with grading in the United States or Canada?

Grade in Your Country	Meaning	North American Equivalent

7. Here are the grades a North American student received. What kind of a student is he? In which areas does he need to improve?

English	C
Math	B
Science	D
Social studies	B
Physical education	A
Spanish	F

8. Work with a partner. One person tells the other what is different about the grading system of his or her country compared with the grading system in North America. The person listening must then repeat this information to his or her partner. Then switch roles. This is a good way to improve your listening skills and learn about another culture.

Matching: Idioms
Here are some idioms commonly used by students in school. Match each idiom with its meaning. (Note: In two cases, two idioms have the same definition.) Check your answers on page 179.

Idiom

_C_ 1. Ace it

_E_ 2. Bomb the test

_J_ 3. brown-nose

_B_ 4. "Mega" homework

_F_ 5. Blow-off course

_J_ 6. Suck up

_H_ 7. Pull an all-nighter

_E_ 8. Flunk

_A_ 9. Killer course

_G_ 10. Data brain

_K_ 11. Hard nose

_L_ 12. Mark on a curve

_D_ 13. Easy grader

Definition

A. A difficult subject
B. A lot of work to do
C. To get an A
D. Gives many good grades
E. To fail an exam
F. An easy course
G. A very smart person
H. To study instead of sleep
I. To fail
J. To try hard to please
K. A difficult teacher
L. To add points to the grades

Role-Play
With a partner, prepare a dialogue for each of the following situations. Be prepared to role-play each of the situations in front of the class.

1. You are away at college and have just received a telephone call telling you that a close relative is very ill. You are upset and can't study. Finally, you decide that you must go home. Role-play your conversation with your teacher, explaining that you must return home.
2. You don't understand the word *invertebrate,* which your biology teacher has been using. Role-play raising your hand and asking what it means. Role-play asking about the term *laissez faire* in social studies and the difference between *induction* and *deduction* in math. The person playing the part of the teacher should look up the word in the dictionary and be able to answer questions about it.
3. You are visiting your child's teacher on parent-teacher conference day. Be prepared to ask how your child is doing: Is your child having any problem with class work? Does your child get along with the other children? Is your child well behaved in class? Think of some more questions to ask.

3 Asking for Help

In the United States and Canada, students are expected to participate actively in their classes. They are expected to ask and answer questions. Students can also ask brief questions in class or see the teacher privately for extra help or lengthier explanations of class material. To ask questions and get information, you need to know the idioms and phrases used to seek information. Please study the following brief dialogues before proceeding. Notice that some are appropriate to the classroom, where you ask questions which would be of interest to the class. Others are used in the privacy of the teacher's office, where you want to discuss something that is related to you personally.

In class:

1. YOU: I'm not sure I understand. Will you please repeat that?

   TEACHER: Yes, I said that . . .

2. YOU: Please say that again more slowly. I didn't get what you said.

   TEACHER: I said . . .

3. YOU: Would you mind rewording that?

   TEACHER: Sure. I said . . .

4. YOU: Excuse me. Do you mean that . . .?

   TEACHER: Yes, that's correct.

In the teacher's office:

1. YOU: Do you have a minute?

   TEACHER: I can't talk right now. How about tomorrow at this time?

   YOU: Fine. See you then.

2. YOU: Can you tell me how I'm doing in class?

   TEACHER: I'd be happy to.

3. YOU: I'm having trouble with the essay. Do you have any suggestions about organization?

   TEACHER: Yes, limit your topic and decide on your main ideas.

   YOU: That's really helpful. I certainly understand it better now. Thank you.

   TEACHER: You're welcome. Come again whenever you need help. See you in class.

4. YOU: How can I improve my work?

   TEACHER: You could . . .

   YOU: What other changes do you suggest?

   TEACHER: I think you should . . .

To a professor's secretary:

YOU: Excuse me.

SECRETARY: Yes, what do you want?

YOU: I need to speak to Professor Miller.

SECRETARY: Just a moment. I'll tell the professor you're here.

Now You Do It   Often students need to ask the teacher questions to find out more about the subject or to help them understand the lesson. Read the following dialogues, and for each compose a question that a student could ask the teacher.

1. The class has been discussing school.

TEACHER: And that's how students act in the United States.

YOU: _____?

TEACHER: That's an excellent question. Can anyone answer it?

CLASSMATE: _____.

TEACHER: Good answer! Can anyone add to her answer?

Notice that in North America, teachers often ask other students in the class to supply the answers to questions instead of always giving the answer themselves.

2. Your class has been discussing major rivers in North America. You want to know how long the Mississippi River is.

YOU: _____?

PROFESSOR: I'm not sure exactly how long the Mississippi River is. Why don't you look it up in the encyclopedia and tell the class tomorrow.

Teachers in the United States and Canada are not uncomfortable saying they don't know the answer to a question. Also, sometimes instead of answering questions, they will encourage students to think for themselves by asking them to find the answer.

3. Students in the United States and Canada are interested in getting high grades. A passing mark of *C* is often not acceptable to them. Students who feel that a grade is unfairly low may ask the instructor why they received a particular grade on a paper and how they can improve their work.

TEACHER: Hello, Jim. Can I help you?

JIM: _____?

TEACHER: The reason you received a low grade was that your paper was not well organized and contained many spelling and grammar mistakes.

JIM: _____?

TEACHER: If you want to improve your organization, make an outline before you write your paper. Read each sentence carefully to find mistakes in grammar and spelling. You may wish to have a friend help you find errors.

JIM: _____.

TEACHER: I'm glad that will help you. Come see me before you hand in your next paper, and we'll go over it together.

Conduct in the classroom in North America may be quite different from behavior you are accustomed to. In the United States and Canada, class participation is often considered important. Teachers respect a student's right to ask questions, and some teachers even play "devil's advocate" (take the opposite position) to encourage students to think for themselves. To do this, instructors use a variety of methods to get information from their students.

In these dialogues, you will find typical questioning techniques North American teachers use. Fill in the dialogue, using the sentences below it. When you finish, check your answers on page 179.

Matching: Model Dialogues

A. A teacher is discussing free speech in a sociology class.

1. TEACHER: Define *free speech*.

   YOU: _____.

2. TEACHER: What do you mean by that?

   YOU: _____.

3. TEACHER: Can you explain it further?

   YOU: _____.

4. TEACHER: Give me an example, please.

   YOU: _____.

3 a. In North America, you can say you disagree with government leaders.
4 b. Even the newspaper can criticize the president or the prime minister.
1 c. Free speech means that people can say whatever they want.
2 d. You can criticize the government and nothing will happen to you.

B. A political science class is studying the United Nations.

1. TEACHER: How has the United Nations changed in the past ten years?

   STUDENT 1: _____.

2. TEACHER: Can anyone help?

   STUDENT 2: _____.

3. TEACHER: Very good. Has the United Nations changed in any other way?

   STUDENT 3: _____.

2 a. More Third World countries belong to the United Nations now.
1 b. I'm not sure.
3 c. Yes, the Third World countries can outvote some of the larger nations.

4 Summary

What's Going On Here?

Below are four situations involving international students in a school setting. In each situation, there is cultural misunderstanding. Read each situation, and then answer the *Discussion Questions* with your classmates.

A. John is an international student who has come to the United States to study engineering. He is failing physics and calculus and getting a *D* in chemistry. He has an *A* in literature and an *A* in music. His college adviser has asked him to come in to talk to him. When they meet, John explains that he studies very hard, but he just can't seem to get good grades in his science and math courses.

His adviser suggests that he change his major, but John says that he can't do that. He must study to become an engineer. When his adviser asks him why, John says that he came to the United States to study engineering, and that is what he must do.

His adviser asks him if he likes the science and math courses and John responds by saying, "What does that have to do with anything?"

John's adviser explains that people tend to do better in courses that they like. He asks John why he thinks he has done so well in literature and music. John explains that he reads a lot. He smiles and says he has always enjoyed reading and that he plays the saxophone, the trumpet, and the piano. In fact, he says "I used to play in a band, but my parents didn't like it so I had to stop."

John promises to do better next semester. His adviser explains that if he doesn't improve his grades next semester, he will flunk out of school. John says that he understands, and he will try harder.

Discussion questions

1. What subjects does John seem to be good at?
2. What subjects is he failing?
3. What conclusion does his adviser come to based on this information?
4. John's adviser wants him to change his major. Do you think this is a good idea? Why or why not? What does John think? Why?
5. Do you think John will do better next semester in his math and science courses? Why?
6. Do you think John is sincere about trying harder next semester? Will that make a difference? Why or why not? Do you think he tried hard this semester?
7. What is the problem?
8. What doesn't John want to accept? Why?
9. What doesn't his adviser understand? Why?

B. Dean Atkins met with an international student who had a *C* average in his master's program. They had the following conversation.

DEAN ATKINS: Mr. Arn, I have called you into my office because your average has fallen below a *B* for the second semester. I'm afraid you will not be allowed to continue your studies at this school.

MR. ARN: I don't understand; I have passed everything.

DEAN ATKINS: Mr. Arn, I explained to you last semester that in graduate school you must maintain a *B* average. Getting *C*s in graduate school is not acceptable.

MR. ARN: But a *C* is a passing grade. What do you mean by saying I can't continue my studies here?

DEAN ATKINS: You are being suspended from school. You may reapply, if you wish, in a year. But you may not study here next year.

MR. ARN: But I have to study here. I must be a full-time student to keep my visa. If I don't study full-time, I will get in trouble with immigration.

DEAN ATKINS: I'm sorry, Mr. Arn. In that case, you will have to go home. We will not let you continue your studies here next year.

MR. ARN: You don't understand. I can't go home! I can't disappoint my parents! I will bring shame to my family!

DEAN ATKINS: There is nothing I can do about that. I will be happy to assist you in finding another school to transfer to if that is what you decide to do. Thank you for coming in to see me. I wish you good luck in your future endeavors.

Discussion questions

1. Why has the dean asked to see Mr. Arn?
2. What does Mr. Arn fail to understand?
3. What does the dean say Mr. Arn can do after a year?
4. Why does Mr. Arn say he can't do that?
5. Why does Mr. Arn say he cannot go home now?
6. What is the dean's position?
7. What are the cultural problems in this encounter?

C. The director of the English Language Program at a university has called Eric into her office.

DIRECTOR: Eric, you have not gotten good grades this semester, and we cannot recommend you to begin academic courses.

ERIC: I don't understand. I passed everything. I worked hard and only bombed two tests. I even aced a physics test.

DIRECTOR: Eric, you received a *D* in all of your courses.

ERIC: I didn't suck up to my teachers and none of my teachers were easy graders. But, anyway, *D* is passing.

DIRECTOR: A grade of *D* is barely passing. Students who receive a D in a course have not adequately proved that they know the material.

ERIC: I don't understand. I took three killer courses and none of my teachers graded on a curve. I pulled all-nighters and did mega homework assignments. Besides, *D* is passing.

DIRECTOR: Yes, it is passing. But it indicates that the student does not know the material well. A student may receive a *D* in one course, and if all the other grades are good, he or she will be allowed to take an academic course or move to the next level. However, you received a *D* in **all** of your courses. Under the circumstances, I cannot let you move to the next level or take any academic courses.

ERIC: That's not fair. I don't understand. I passed everything. You just don't like me because I'm not a data brain and I refuse to be a brown-nose.

DIRECTOR: That isn't so. Liking you has nothing to do with it. You will have to do better next semester.

Discussion questions.

1. Why has the director asked to see Eric?
2. Why does Eric say he has passed all his courses?
3. Why does the director say that *D*s aren't acceptable?
4. Why does Eric say that the director doesn't like him?
5. What are the cultural problems?

D. Mindy had heard when she was in her home country that North American teachers are very relaxed, that they tell jokes and call students by their first name. She had also heard that teachers dress informally. She thought it would be fun to study in the United States, but she wasn't prepared for what happened to her the first week in class.

On her first day at school, Mindy was surprised to see her teacher sitting on the desk. Her teacher told the students her name was Barbara and when Mindy said, "Miss Barbara, what is the homework assignment?" Barbara laughed and said, "My first name is Barbara. I am Barbara Kelly. Just call me Barbara. We never use Mr., Miss, or Mrs. with a first name." Everyone laughed. Mindy felt uncomfortable.

The next day they were talking about differences between cultures. Each student had to tell something that he or she would never say when meeting people for the first time.

One student, Ann, said that she would never ask people how old they were. Another student, Jennifer, said she wouldn't ask people how much money they made. Then the teacher asked Mindy what people couldn't say in her country. Mindy thought for a minute and she said, "We can say anything in my country."

The teacher looked at her and said, "Could you say, 'My, you have a fat mother!' Everyone laughed. Mindy's face turned red and she looked down at the ground.

Barbara said, laughingly, "Well, could you say that?" She looked kindly at Mindy with a big smile on her face, but Mindy didn't see her because she was looking at the floor.

Mindy didn't answer and kept looking down. The class was still laughing. Finally, Mindy whispered "No."

The next day, Mindy went to the registrar's office and dropped Barbara's class. She really wanted to go home.

Discussion questions

1. What did Mindy know about North America before she came?
2. What happened on her first day at school that made her feel uncomfortable? Was she justified in feeling that way?
3. Would you have felt uncomfortable in that situation?
4. What was the cultural problem?
5. How could this situation have been avoided?
6. What could Mindy or the teacher have done to correct the situation? Could it be corrected or was it too late?

Exploring North America

In this exercise you will have an opportunity to explore how North Americans act in a variety of situations.

A. Ask five North American students these questions and be prepared to discuss their responses with your class.

1. Why did you choose to attend college (or high school)?
2. How did you decide what to study in school? Who helped you make your choice?
3. Do your parents approve of the subjects you're studying? What would you do if they wanted you to study something you didn't want to study?

4. What are the characteristics of an outstanding teacher?
5. Who has the ultimate responsibility for learning in the classroom, the teacher or the student? Why?

B. Observe several classes in your school to learn the following information. Discuss your findings with your class.

1. How do students dress to attend class?
2. How do faculty members dress to attend class?
3. What is the relationship between the faculty members and the students? Give specific details—examples—to support your answer.
4. How do faculty members deal with disruptive students in the classroom?
5. Do faculty members allow students to ask questions and to express their opinions?
6. What do faculty members do when a student gives the wrong answer?
7. List three differences you have observed between classroom conduct and teaching methods in the United States or Canada and in your country.

Speaking Out In this exercise you will be given more information about attending school and asked to discuss it.

A. In the United States and Canada any student who has graduated from high school may attend college. Although many colleges are very selective, some colleges admit all students who apply, even those who are not academically prepared to do the work. For these students, they offer special remedial classes which are designed to teach them the skills they need to succeed in college. Some colleges even give students college credit for attending these courses.

1. Do you think that anyone who wishes to go to college should be allowed to attend? Why or why not? What are the standards for admitting students into college in your country? Which standard for admission do you prefer? Why?
2. Do you think that colleges should offer remedial courses to help students remedy academic deficiencies? Why or why not? Does your school offer courses like these? Do you think that students should get college credit for these courses? Why or why not?
3. As you discussed in "What's Going On Here?" on page 39, some college and high school teachers conduct their classes informally. Some allow their students to call them by their first names, do not have firm deadlines for work, and encourage students to openly disagree with their statements about the subject and with their teaching methods. How do you feel about this? Under what circumstances would these teaching approaches be acceptable? Why?

B. In the United States, college grades are sent directly to the student, although the parents may have paid the tuition and the student is a minor. Colleges will not even discuss the student's progress with the parents without the student's permission. Do you agree with this policy? Discuss your answer with the class. How do colleges interact with the parents of students in your country?

C. When North American students strongly disagree with a school or government policy, they hold "demonstrations" to voice their opposition. For example, many American students demonstrated against the war in Vietnam, for civil rights, or for the legalization of marijuana. These demonstrations often include taking over buildings, carrying signs and chanting slogans, and blocking classrooms so that other students and faculty cannot attend class. Sometimes, demonstrators threaten to commit acts of violence unless their demands are met.

Under what circumstances should students be allowed to demonstrate? Why? Should students' demands be met because of threats of violence? What should a college or government do in such cases? Under what circumstances would you participate in a demonstration? Why?

three

Building Friendships

Some people, when they first arrive in North America, say that Americans and Canadians are very friendly, but after living there for a while, they change their minds. One international student explained that when he first came, people were very friendly. They helped him get settled, took him shopping, invited him for dinner, and called to see how he was. After two or three weeks, however, they stopped doing these things, and he was confused and disappointed.

North Americans tend to do what is necessary to help people when they first arrive. They "go all out" doing many things to help new arrivals get settled and often make them feel like part of the family. The newcomers expect this warm hospitality to continue in the form of a solid friendship. However, North Americans expect that once people are settled and have been there for a few weeks, they will begin to do things for themselves and become independent.

Like other aspects of culture, friendship is perceived differently in various parts of the world. In this chapter, we will discuss friends, neighbors, and acquaintances. We will talk about how to make friends in North America and how to communicate with them during both troublesome and happy times. As we discuss friendship in the United States and Canada, compare it with friendship as it is experienced in your culture. Share this information with your classmates.

1 Friendships Across Cultures

Analysis   The word *friend* in North America has a broad meaning, including everyone from a casual acquaintance to a long-time best friend. The following chart describes some of these levels of friendship.

Term	Definition	Customary Behavior
Neighbor	Someone who lives next door, across the street, or on the same block	Neighbors generally say hello when they see each other. Some become good friends. They often help each other, borrow things, and watch each other's houses when no one is home.
Acquaintance	Someone you have been introduced to but do not know well	Acquaintances generally say hello when they meet and make small talk.
Best friend	Someone you can rely on and of whom you would feel comfortable asking for assistance at any time	Best friends generally share good and bad times together and spend free time together.
Boyfriend/girlfriend	Someone of the opposite sex for whom you have romantic feelings	People go on dates, share affection, and walk arm in arm in public with their boyfriends or girlfriends.
Girlfriend	A female friend of another woman (*boyfriend* not used by men and boys to refer to their male friends)	Girlfriends spend time together and share common interests.
Classmate	A student in your class	Classmates say hello, make small talk, and sometimes study together.
Business associate or colleague	Someone who works in the same place of business as you do	Colleagues share business information, discuss problems related to their work, and occasionally socialize.

Let's Share   After studying the chart above, complete this *Let's Share*.

1. Describe the type of relationship people in your country have with the following people.

Neighbors: _____

_____

_____

Acquaintances: _____

_____

_____

Best friends: _____

_____

_____

Boyfriends/
girlfriends: _____

_____

_____

2. Are there other categories of friendship in your culture? Please explain. Share this information with fellow class members.

_____

_____

_____

3. Now that you have discussed friends and the different levels of friendship, take a few minutes to think about your friends at home in your country.

Working in pairs, find out from your partner the answers to the following questions:

a. Who is you partner's best friend?
b. What makes this friend so special?
c. Was there one thing this friend did that showed him or her to be a true friend?
d. What does your partner remember best about this friend?
e. What was an especially important experience that your partner shared with this special friend?

When you have finished, report to the class the answers to questions 2 and 3. Are there any similarities or differences in people's answers to these questions? Do different cultures view and deal with friendship in unique ways?

In chapter 1 we talked about body language and gestures. Now let's consider your image—that is, the way you appear to others. Clothes, hairstyles, makeup, cleanliness, posture, and even a person's name tell you a great deal about someone.

Look at the pictures below and decide how you feel about each person. Use the questions on the next page as a guide:

A B C

D E

F

G

1. Would you like to have this person as a friend or relative? Why or why not?
2. What do you think the person in the photograph is like? Consider descriptions like **fun loving, proper, educated, respected, well behaved, poor, honest, friendly, weak, sad.** What gives you this impression?
3. In English we have these expressions: "Clothes make the man" and "You can't tell a book by its cover." Do you agree with these sayings? Why or why not?

Let's Share   Now answer these questions:

1. What personal characteristics do people in your culture admire and respect (for example, dress, appearance, friendliness)?
2. What is your idea of a "beautiful" person? Discuss this person's physical, intellectual, and emotional characteristics. Form groups of three and discuss the ways that your ideals are the same or different. Why do people have different ideas of beauty?
3. How do stereotypes limit our opportunities to meet and learn from other people and situations.

Hygiene   As you have just seen, appearance plays an important part, rightly or wrongly, in the way we feel about people. Therefore, it is very important to make a good first impression. However, the feeling that people get when meeting one another for the first time is not just based on how they look.

Look at the items on this list. What do they have in common?

Spray deodorant
Roll-on deodorant
Breath mints
Chewing gum
Mouthwash

All of these products are used to prevent body odors. North Americans are offended if a person smells of sweat or has bad breath. Showering daily, as most North Americans do, is not sufficient to prevent body odor (or **B.O.**, as it is called). Because North Americans are so sensitive to odor, they use a deodorant under their arms, brush their teeth twice a day, and use breath fresheners when they believe their breath smells stale, after smoking or after eating onions or garlic. Clothes, especially shirts and blouses, are washed after one or two wearings, even if they appear to be clean.

47

Let's Share   The senses of sight, smell, taste, touch, and hearing play an important role in how we perceive another culture. (Remember the optical illusions in chapter 1 and our discussion of perception.) List the sights, sounds, tastes, and smells that remind you most strongly of your family or hometown.

1. Sights: _____

_____

2. Sounds: _____

_____

3. Tastes: _____

_____

4. Smells: _____

_____

3   Sharing Good and Bad Times

Friends are people with whom we share both good and bad times. We share happiness, excitement, anxiety, and sadness with them. This chapter is made up of exercises and conversations that contain idioms and expressions used to convey and share these emotions. In this section, you will be asked to work with a partner to develop dialogues based on particular situations in which these feelings are expressed.

Excitement   Sharing your joys and happiness is one of the most pleasant parts of friendship. The conversations that follow contain many expressions commonly used to express excitement.

Model Dialogues

1. PERSON A: I can't believe it! I got an *A* on my science test!

   PERSON B: Congratulations! That's great!

   A: Thanks. I'm so happy! I really worked hard for that *A*.

   B: I know you did. You deserve it.

2. A: I have the most wonderful news!

   B: What happened?

   A: My sister finally had a baby girl. It's great, because she has three boys!

   B: How wonderful!

3. A: You'll never believe this!

   B: What happened?

A: I won five dollars in the school raffle! How about that!

B: Boy, are you lucky!

Form groups of four or five. As a group, come up with two situations that would cause excitement. Then write a dialogue to go with each situation. After your teacher has checked your work, role-play them for the class. Be sure to use gestures, body language, and facial expressions as well as words to convey your meaning.

Worry is a common feeling and one that can be alleviated by sharing with friends. People respond to worry in many ways. Some people become irritable, others become very quietand intense, and still others may become sad and distracted. Look at the photograph below. It shows a person who is worried. Notice her gestures, body language, and facial expression. What makes this person look worried?

Model Dialogues

Here are some ways to express and respond to worry.

1. PERSON A: I'm so upset.

   PERSON B: What's the matter? What happened?

2. A: I really need to talk to you. Do you have a minute?

   B: Sure. What's bothering you?

3. **A:** I have a real problem. I don't know what to do!

   B: What is the trouble? How can I help you?

Role Play

Read these sample dialogues. Then, using correct gestures, facial expressions, and bodylanguage, role-play them with a partner.

JANE: What's wrong? You really look worried and upset.

SARAH: My dog was hit by a car.

JANE: That's terrible! Is he okay?

SARAH: I don't know. He's at the vet's.

JANE: I hope he'll be all right.

SARAH: Thank you. So do I.

TOM: I'm so worried. I haven't heard from my family in three months.

ADAM: How often do they usually write?

TOM: Oh, at least once a month. Either my mother or my father writes.

ADAM: The mail is really slow sometimes. I'm sure you'll hear from them soon.

TOM: I hope so.

ADAM: You know the saying, "No news is good news." If something were wrong, they'd have contacted you.

TOM: Maybe you're right. Thanks, Adam.

Talking It Over

With whom do people in your country talk about their family, financial, or personal problems? With your classmates, discuss when they talk about their problems to one of the following:

a teacher	a member of the clergy (priest, minister, rabbi, guru, or
a parent	other religious leader)
a friend	a doctor
a neighbor	a psychiatrist
a school counselor	a stranger
a social worker	a psychologist

4   Problem Situations

Sometimes you will find yourself in a situation that requires you to act in a way that is contrary to what your friends want or believe is correct. These situations are often difficult to handle. You will find it helpful first to analyze the situation, decide how strongly you feel about it, and then act.

Quick Customs Quiz

On the next page are situations in which you might find yourself when you are in the United States or Canada. Read each situation, decide what is appropriate, and choose the answer that best fits the circumstance. Draw a circle around the letter in front of your answer. Check your answers against those on page 179, which are the answers an

American or a Canadian would probably give. When you have checked your answers, discuss them with your class. Then role-play each situation with another member of your class.

1. Your neighbor is playing his stereo very loudly. It is three o'clock in the morning and the music is keeping you awake. What should you do?

   a. Shout for him to turn it down.
   b. Bang on the wall.
   c. Call him on the telephone and politely ask him to turn it down.
   d. Do nothing. He can do what he wants—it's a free country.
   e. Call the police.
   f. Call the landlord.
   g. Play your stereo just as loud.

2. At a party, your friend offers you marijuana or cocaine. When you politely refuse, he says, "Aw, come on! Everyone does it!" How should you handle this situation?

   a. Give him a lecture on the dangers of using drugs.
   b. Say, "Thanks, but I'd rather not."
   c. Say, "Nobody but a real fool would use drugs, and you're obviously a fool." Then walk away.
   d. Ask him if his parents know that he is using drugs.
   e. Accept the drugs so that you will be considered a friend.

3. You are an excellent student and carefully prepare your homework every night. Your friend is having trouble in class and asks to copy your work. What should you do?

   a. Let her copy your work.
   b. Help by showing her how to do the homework but not letting her copy your work.
   c. Refuse.
   d. Tell your professor.

4. You were assigned a roommate at your college. After living with that person for several weeks, you do not wish to live with her anymore. She is rude, messy, noisy, and inconsiderate. What should you do?

   a. Be rude, messy, noisy, and inconsiderate.
   b. Ask the housing authorities for another room and move out.
   c. Make her life miserable so that she will ask for another room and move out.
   d. Nothing. It will be too embarrassing to admit that you can't get along with your roommate.
   e. Tell her how you feel and work out a solution with her.

5. You have recently come to North America and don't know many people. When you tell a friend that you would like to meet someone of the opposite sex, your friend offers to "fix you up with a blind date." What does he mean by this?

   a. He wants to introduce you to someone you don't know and have you go with this person on a date.
   b. He thinks that there is something wrong with you and wants you to go out with someone who can't see.
   c. He wants you to go on a date with someone who can't see.
   d. He wants you to go to a party where the lights are extremely dim.

Now You Do It With a partner, choose one item from each question and develop a dialogue. After the instructor checks your dialogue, role-play it for the class.

1. Choose a happy situation from one of those below or add one of your own.

   a. You have just become an aunt or an uncle.
   b. You received an *A* on an English essay.
   c. You have been offered a job at which you will be earning $15 an hour.
   d. You meet a friend you haven't seen in ten years.

2. Choose a tense situation from the list that follows. Write a dialogue in which a friend uses conversational skills to find out what is wrong and then is helpful and reassuring.

   a. You are worried about failing math.
   b. Your family hasn't written or called in a long time.
   c. Your 16-year-old sister wants to get married.
   d. You lost your job.
   e. You lost $50 from your wallet.
   f. The immigration officer wants to see you.

3. Choose one of the awkward situations below.

   a. Explain to your friend that he cannot bring his dog to the picnic with him.
   b. Your friend has introduced you to a friend of his and hopes that you will like each other. You go on a "blind date" and find that you cannot get along. Tell your friend about it in a nice way.
   c. You are living with a person who will not do his or her share of the housework. Persuade this person to do the dishes since you have done the cooking for the evening and it is his or her turn to clean up.
   d. Drinking is against your religion; however, at a party, someone offers you a drink. This person does not mean to insult you. Refuse in a polite way.

5 Summary

Read the situations described below and, using the cultural information you have learned in this chapter, figure out what the problem was and how it could have been avoided.

What's Going On Here? A. Look at the cartoons below and read the captions. Then, with your classmates, answer the *Discussion Questions*.

Discussion questions

1. What do the visitors bring?
2. Who made it?
3. What do they say about their gift?
4. How does this make the hosts feel?
5. What does the host finally do?
6. Would you have thrown the cake away? Do you think it was terrible or unsafe to eat?
7. Why did the visitors talk that way about their gift?

B. Here is a typical cultural misunderstanding involving attitudes toward friendship. Read about the situation, and then answer the *Discussion Questions* with your classmates.

Marie and Jennifer had been neighbors for three months when Marie became really upset with Jennifer. When they first moved in and got to know each other, they did everything together. They went grocery shopping together, explored the neighborhood, took walks, and went to the movies on Friday evenings. They spent a lot of time in each other's apartments just talking.

Now Jennifer seems to have made other friends. Sometimes she includes Marie, butoften she goes out and doesn't ask Marie to join her. Jennifer can't understand what happened to their friendship.

Marie thought that Jennifer was the perfect example of how unfriendly Americans could be. They make you think that they like you and then all of a sudden they're not your friend any more.

In fact, now, when Marie drops in on Jennifer, Jennifer says things like, "Oh, Marie it's nice to see you, but I can't talk for long. I have an appointment in a few minutes."

Jennifer said she couldn't take Marie to the airport or pick her up when she came back because she was busy. She even seemed annoyed that Jennifer had asked!

Marie thought that was terrible. After all, what are friends for if not to help you when you need them?

Discussion questions

1. Why did Marie and Jennifer spend so much time together at first? Why don't they spend as much time together now?
2. Has Marie made other friends since she moved there? Has Jennifer made other friends since she moved there? Why do you think that is the case?
3. Do you think Jennifer is no longer interested in being Marie's friend?
4. What did Marie ask Jennifer to do for her? Why was Jennifer upset with that request?
5. Why was Marie upset that Jennifer said she couldn't take her to the airport or pick her up when she returned?
6. Do you think each thinks of the other as a friend? How do their definitions of *friend* differ?

C. Read about the misunderstanding between Jim and Mrs. Jones. Then, with your classmates, answer the questions that follow.

Mrs. Jones was a foreign-student adviser at Jim's university. Jim, who had always paid his tuition on time, was two months late with his payment.

Mrs. Jones called Jim into her office and asked him why he hadn't paid. She thought perhaps there was a problem getting the money out of his country because that difficulty had arisen before.

Jim said that that wasn't the problem. Actually, the money had arrived on time—all $4,000—but he didn't have it now. He had lent it to a friend to buy a car.

Mrs. Jones wanted to know who Jim's friend was, but he couldn't tell her his name. Mrs. Jones thought that Jim was lying to her. It didn't seem reasonable, first, that he would lend someone so much money and, second, that he would forget the name of the person he had given it to. She became angry and accused Jim of making up the story.

Jim was insulted. He had always had a good relationship with Mrs. Jones. How could she think he would lie to her? He told her that his roommate, from his home country, had a friend at another school whose car was damaged in an accident—so he couldn't get to school. He needed money to buy a car, or he would be in trouble with immigration for not going to school. What could he do? He had to give his roommate the money for his friend. After all, they came from the same country!

Mrs. Jones should have been proud of his loyalty to his friend, thought Jim. Instead, she was angry, and he couldn't understand why.

Mrs. Jones thought the whole story was crazy. Who would give money, especially so much, to a total stranger? Jim must be lying. She was very upset, and she told Jim that if he didn't pay his tuition by the end of the week, he would have to leave school.

Discussion questions

1. Was Jim telling the truth?
2. Why didn't Mrs. Jones believe him?
3. Would you lend so much money to a friend? To someone you didn't know if a friend asked you to?
4. What is the problem here?

D. Now read about the misunderstanding between Scott and his teacher, Mr. Davidson. Then, with your class, answer the questions below.

Mike Davidson cared very much about his students, and they all liked him very much. He wanted them to learn, and he wanted them to be happy. He had a special relationship with one student, Scott. Scott had been to his house several times and had come to know Mr. Davidson's wife and children.

Now, Mr. Davidson was very worried about Scott because the student's country had recently erupted into war. Mr. Davidson observed that Scott had lost a lot of weight and that he had dark circles under his eyes. He talked to Scott and was as supportive as he could be, but he felt that in this situation, Scott should see a professional, a doctor or a counselor.

After class one day, Mr. Davidson spoke to Scott and suggested that he go to the counseling center on campus to talk to one of the psychologists there. Or, he said, Scott might go to the health center and talk to one of the doctors.

Scott's face became very red. He said, "I don't need a doctor or a psychologist. What's the matter with you? How could you make such a suggestion? I thought you were my friend!"

Mr. Davidson was very surprised by Scott's reaction. He said, "I'm sorry to have upset you so much. I just wanted to help."

Since they had that conversation, Scott has stopped talking to Mr. Davidson. He has also transferred out of his class.

Discussion questions

1. What kind of relationship did Scott and Mr. Davidson have before Scott became upset with his teacher?
2. Why was Mr. Davidson worried about Scott? How did Scott look?
3. What did Mr. Davidson suggest Scott do?
4. How did Scott feel about the suggestion? Why did it upset him?
5. Why did Scott transfer out of Mr. Davidson's class?
6. What was the reason for the conflict in the story? Was Scott justified in feeling the way he did?

Exploring North America

Investigate North American culture by interviewing people, doing research, and learning as much as you can about the topic presented.

A. A person's "nickname," the special name given by family or friends, can tell a great deal about the person. In the United States and Canada, nicknames are common. For instance, a man may call his son "Junior" instead of his given name. Some nicknames relate to a person's size. For example, a small person may be called a "half-pint" and a large person may be called "Moose."

1. Ask your American or Canadian friends about their nicknames and how they got them.
2. Find out if there are special rules for using nicknames. For example, you may wish to find answers to these questions.

   a. When should a person use his or her nickname? When is using a nickname inappropriate?
   b. Who can call a person by his or her nickname?
   c. There are many "generic" nicknames that people use, such as *honey, dear, friend,* or *buddy.* When is it appropriate to use these nicknames? What should you do if a stranger addresses you by these names?

3. Many North American celebrities, especially sports stars, have special nicknames. Look in magazines or watch television shows to discover several examples. How do you think the celebrity got his or her nickname?

B. It has been said that men and women make friends differently and for different reasons. For example, a woman will choose a friend who is much like herself, so that they can share many feelings, activities, and interests. Men, however, make friends with other men because they share a particular interest or like to do a certain activity. They have nothing in common but their enjoyment of fishing or gardening. He will choose other friends to do other things with.

1. Do you agree with these statements? Why? Give examples from your own experience.
2. Ask your North American friends if they agree with these statements. Share their answers with the class.

C. How do conversations between women differ—in content and style—from conversations between men? How does the conversation change when someone of the opposite sex enters the discussion?

Speaking Out In this exercise you will have an opportunity to further explore friendships in North America.

A. North Americans place great emphasis on youth and physical beauty. Both men and women color their hair to make themselves look younger or more attractive. Men wear wigs or have hair implants to hide the fact that they are losing their hair as they get older. Girls often begin to wear makeup when they are 11 or 12 years old and have "perms" ("permanent" waves or curls are put in the hair). Men and boys wear jewelry, and sometimes they wear earrings in one ear.

1. Do you think that men and women should color their hair? Why or why not?
2. At what age should girls begin to wear makeup? Why?
3. How much makeup should a woman of 18 wear? A woman of 40? A woman of 65?
4. Should a man wear makeup or wear an earring? Why or why not? Under what circumstances is it okay?
5. Why do you think that people in North America are so conscious of their appearance? What does this tell you about North American culture and attitudes?

B. In North America, most young people begin to go on chaperoned dates when they are 13 or 14 years old. Some, however, are allowed to go on dates when they are as young as 10 years old. Young teenagers usually go to parties, movies, dances, or sports events and are taken to these events by their parents. When teenagers are 15 or 16 years old, they are usually allowed to date unchaperoned. Many are allowed to stay out until 1:00 or 2:00 A.M. Some teenagers have their own cars and go where they wish without their parents' permission.

After a friendship becomes "serious," the young couple may decide to "go steady," which means that they agree to date each other exclusively. Some children begin to "go steady" or "see each other" when they are as young as 12 years old.

1. Examine programs on U.S. or Canadian television and advertisements in magazines which encourage young people to form romantic attachments. How old are the couples in the programs and advertisements? What products are being advertised? What is the message of the advertisement? Do the products advertised have anything to do with succeeding in a romantic relationship? Discuss several examples in class.
2. Ask your North American friends to tell you the answers to these questions. Then answer them from your own point of view:

    a. When do you think that people should begin to date? Do you think that people are encouraged to date to form serious relationships at too young an age? Why?
    b. Do you think that "going steady" when you are in junior or senior high school is a good idea? Why or why not?

3. Consider the list of traits below. Which do you consider the ten most important when you are choosing (1) a friend of the same sex, (2) a friend of the opposite sex, and (3) your future husband or wife. Compare your answers with those of a North American friend. Share your answers with the class.

a. Intelligent	i. Likes to do the things I do
b. Compassionate/kind	j. Has the same religious beliefs I do
c. A good conversationalist	k. Well educated
d. Trustworthy	l. Comes from a good family
e. Respects other people	m. Has a good job or income
f. Works hard	n. Polite/uses good manners
g. Has my parents' approval	o. Cares about me for who I am
h. Has the same background and values I do	p. Physically attractive

C. Television talk shows are popular in the United States and Canada; especially popular are those which discuss intimate topics. It is not uncommon for talk-show hosts to encourage their guests or audience members to discuss their sex lives, problems with their marriage or family, or shocking experiences they have had. They also discuss controversial topics such as homosexuality, abortion, drug use, AIDS, child pornography, and political scandals. People on these programs often show graphic examples or photographs, use vulgar language, or get into arguments with other participants on the show.

1. Watch several talk shows on television and note what was discussed, who participated, and how the host controlled the discussion.
2. Discuss these questions: Why do talk-show participants discuss such intimate topics? Why are people willing to reveal personal information about themselves and others on camera?

Four

Dating

In the United States and Canada, individuals have great freedom and opportunity to meet others. People from other countries are sometimes shocked to see how Americans behave. They often go on unsupervised dates in their early teens, share expenses on dates, and even live together without being married. From what you see on television and in the movies, you might be led to believe that "anything goes." This is not the case, however, because North Americans have rules for dating and relationships, even if they don't seem apparent. In this chapter, we will discuss the North American concept of dating. You will have the opportunity to compare these concepts with those of your country.

1 Dating Across Cultures

Relationships between men and women, boys and girls are different all over the world. In some countries, families arrange a marriage before the bride and groom meet; in other countries, the young people select their own male and female friends, go on dates, and then tell their families whom they wish to marry.

Exploring North America The items listed below define dating relationships and customs. Interview North American students to get answers to each question. Then indicate whether this practice is the same or different in your country. If it is different, explain your custom.

Question	In the United States or Canada	In Your Country
1. How do people meet individuals to date?		
2. What characteristics do you look for in the person you want to date? For example, do you consider religion, race, ethnic background, age, physical characteristics? What else?		

Box continued on the following page

Box continued from the preceding page

Question	In the United States or Canada	In Your Country
3. What role do parents have in selecting the person their child will date?		
4. Who invites the other person to a party or other social function?		
5. At what age do people begin to date?		
6. What kinds of things do you do on a date?		

Box continued on the following page

Question	In the United States or Canada	In Your Country
7. Who pays for the date? Under what circumstances?		
8. How much intimacy is expected on the first date? After three or four dates? After six months of dating?		
9. Under what circumstances do an unmarried couple live together? How do people feel about unmarried people living together?		
10. Under what circumstances should an individual visit the apartment of a friend of the opposite sex? What is the possible expectation if you do?		

Matching: Idioms and Expressions These idioms and expressions will help you understand the dating scene in the United States and Canada. See how many you know by matching the idioms and expressions with their definitions. Check your answers on page 179.

_____ 1. Double date

_____ 2. To share expenses, to go "Dutch treat"

_____ 3. Blind date

_____ 4. To make a pass, to come on to someone

_____ 5. To go steady, to go with someone

_____ 6. To feed someone a line

_____ 7. To make out

_____ 8. To go all the way, to score, to come across

_____ 9. To have an affair

_____ 10. To get picked up

_____ 11. To be stood up

_____ 12. To brush someone off

_____ 13. To be seeing someone

_____ 14. Singles bar

A. To form a sexual friendship

B. To meet someone (usually with sexual intent) without having been formally introduced

C. To date someone on an exclusive basis

D. To have sexual intercourse

E. To have each person pay his or her own way

F. A place where unmarried couples go to meet each other

G. A date on which two couples go out together

H. To date someone over a period of time but not necessarily exclusively

I. To mislead someone, especially to persuade that person to have a sexual relationship

J. To kiss passionately

K. A date, arranged by a third party, for two people who have not met

L. To make sexual advances toward a person, usually a woman, either to flatter her or to take advantage of her

M. To have your date fail to appear at the appointed time or even to call to cancel the date

N. To reject or to show a lack of interest in someone

2 Dating Customs

Sometimes when people visit another country, they are surprised by what appears to be a lack of rules. This feeling is particularly noticeable when they try to understand the relationships between men and women.

Quick Customs Quiz Below are situations in which you might find yourself in the United States or Canada. Read each situation, decide what is appropriate, and choose the answer that best fits the circumstance. Draw a circle around the letter in front of your answer. Check your answers against those on page 179, which are the answers an American or a Canadian would probably give. (There may be more than one correct answer.)

1. You are a young woman at a party. A man across the room catches your eye and smiles. You think he looks pleasant, and you would like to meet him. What should you do?

    a. Turn your eyes away.
    b. Go to a group of your friends and ignore him.
    c. Smile.
    d. Get angry because he is so rude.

2. You are a young man in a cafeteria at school. You see a young woman you would like to meet. What should you do?

    a. Make noises and follow her.
    b. Go up to her and tell her she is beautiful.
    c. Pinch her.
    d. Ignore her.
    e. Catch her eye and smile.

3. A young woman is on a date. Her date says, "Let's go to my place." What does that usually mean?

    a. He wants her to go to his apartment and have sex with him.
    b. He wants her to meet his parents.
    c. He is very proud of his apartment and wants to show it to her.

4. You have gone out with someone four or five times, and you like the person very much. What touching in public is acceptable?

    a. None.
    b. Holding hands.
    c. The man may put his arm around the woman's shoulder or waist.
    d. Kissing hello and good-bye on the lips.
    e. Passionate kissing.

5. Where do people usually go on a date?

    a. the movies
    b. dinner
    c. for dessert or a light snack
    d. bowling
    e. the beach
    f. party
    g. theater
    h. roller skating
    i. sporting events

6. When you go on a date, should you bring your date a present?

    a. Yes
    b. Only if it is a special occasion such as a prom.

7. If a man asks a woman to go to the movies or to dinner, who should pay?

    a. They should split the bill.
    b. The woman should pay.
    c. The man should pay.
    d. It depends on the circumstances.

8. When arrangements are made to go on a date, where does the couple usually meet?

    a. They meet at the restaurant or theater.
    b. The man picks up the woman at her home.
    c. It depends on the circumstances.

Model Dialogues   Here are some conversation models in which people invite someone of the opposite sex to go out on a date or to a party. Practice these models with a classmate.

1. JIM: Hi, Susan.

    SUSAN: Hi, Jim.

    JIM: I was wondering if you were doing anything Friday night. I have tickets to a rock concert.

    SUSAN: Which one?

    JIM: I have two tickets to see the Flaming Idiots concert. Would you like to go with me?

    SUSAN: I'd love to!

    JIM: Great! I'll pick you up at seven o'clock.

    SUSAN: Okay. See you then.

    JIM: Good-bye.

2. LAURIE: Hi, Jeff.

    JEFF: How's it going?

    LAURIE: Great. I'm having a party Saturday night and I'd like you to come.

    JEFF: Thanks. What time does it start?

    LAURIE: Eight-thirty. Can you come?

    JEFF: Sure, I wouldn't miss one of your parties.

3. JULIE: Hi, Alex.

    ALEX: Oh, Julie. You're just the person I wanted to see!

    JULIE: Really? What's up?

    ALEX: How would you like to go to next Saturday's football game with me?

    JULIE: Next Saturday? Gee, I'm sorry. I can't. That's my mother's birthday.

    ALEX: Oh, I was really hoping you could go.

    JULIE: Well, maybe some other time.

The third conversation is particularly important because the person who is being invited has politely declined the invitation. Julie has given a good reason for saying that she can't go to the game and is letting Alex know that perhaps she would be interested in going with him another time.

There are two other ways in which she could have handled the situation, however. If she really **did** want to go out with Alex and wanted to express her interest strongly, she could have declined in this manner:

ALEX: Oh, I was really hoping you could go.

JULIE: Yes, me, too. **How about the game on the following Saturday?**

ALEX: That's a great idea! I'll call you later in the week and we can decide on when to go and what to do after the game.

Julie makes her willingness clear by suggesting an alternative. Sometimes you really don't want to date a person but wish to avoid hurting that person's feelings. Let's consider how Julie could have handled the situation if she did not want to go on a date with Alex:

ALEX: Oh, I was really hoping you could go.

JULIE: **Thank you for asking me anyway.**

Here Julie politely declines the invitation and thanks Alex for asking her but does not indicate that she would like to go out another time.

Now You Do It   In groups of three, write a dialogue for the following situations. Take turns having two people role-play the situation while one student observes and comments on how it was handled.

1. You wish to ask someone to your party on Saturday. After the other person accepts, you provide details about when and where it will be held and who will be attending.
2. Someone asks you on a date. You don't want to go but don't wish to hurt the person's feelings. You don't want to have the person ask you out again.
3. You have been asked to a party and cannot attend because you must baby-sit. Decline, but let the other person know that you would like to be invited some other time.
4. You and your friend have decided to spend Saturday evening together. Decide where you'll go, what you'll do, and when you'll meet.
5. Someone you like has invited you to go to the drive-in, an outdoor theater where you watch the movie from your car. You prefer to go to movies in an indoor theater. Discuss this with your date and suggest going to an indoor theater.

3   Compliments and Conversation

Now that you have made arrangements to go out, what will you talk about on your date? Most people begin with small talk such as the weather and then move on to areas of mutual interest. It is common to compliment your date. Here are some ways to give and to accept compliments.

1. TED: Hi. You look great!

   KATHY: Thank you, Ted.

2. LISA: That's a nice jacket, Bob.

   BOB: Thanks. I bought it just for this occasion.

3. CYNTHIA: I like your tie. Is it new?

   JERRY: Yes. Glad you like it. I got it for my birthday.

Now You Do It   If the dating customs in your country are different from those practiced in the United States or Canada, you may want to talk about these differences with your date. In the following conversation, an international student is on a blind date. As a topic of conversation, he mentions that people do not go on blind dates in his country. That leads to a conversation about dating customs and other areas of discussion. Complete this conversation as you would if you were the person on the blind date. Then role-play it with a class member.

YOU: This is my first blind date. We don't do this in my country.

DATE: What do you do to meet people?

YOU: _____

_____.

DATE: That's very interesting. But what if _____

_____.

YOU: _____

_____.

DATE: Do you have singles bars or dating services?

YOU: _____

_____.

DATE: How old are people when they begin to go out on dates in your country?

YOU: _____

_____.

DATE: What kinds of things do people do on dates?

YOU: _____

_____.

DATE: Your country sounds like an interesting place. I'd like to visit there sometime. What do you think that I should do when I go to your country?

YOU: _____

_____.

DATE: This country seems very different from _____. Are there any customs that I should know before I get there so that I won't offend anyone?

YOU: _____

_____.

DATE: That's good to know! I'd never have thought of that.

YOU: Well, are you ready to go to the movie now?

DATE: _____

_____.

66

When the date is over, it is customary for the man to take the woman home. They thank each other for an enjoyable evening. Sometimes on a first date, a couple may kiss good night if they like each other.

SUE: Thank you for a lovely evening.

JOE: I had a great time, too. I'll call you this week and maybe we can go out again next weekend.

SUE: Yes, I'd like that. Good night, Joe.

JOE: (leans over and kisses her) Good night, Sue.

Notice that in this conversation, Joe indicates that he would like to date Sue again, and she agrees.

Role-Play Form groups of three or four people. Discuss how you would handle each of the following situations. Then take turns acting out the situations while other group members observe. The observers should notice the body language and facial expressions of the actors as well as their words.

1. You wish to ask someone on a date to go to the football game at the local college. Choose a partner and make arrangements. (The other person may accept or refuse.)
2. You are a young woman who is at a party alone. A young man comes up to you and makes a pass. Handle the situation tactfully.
3. You are at a party and see someone you would like to meet. Role-play two ways of meeting this person. After you meet, carry on small talk for three minutes.
4. You don't know anyone in town and tell a friend that you would like to meet someone nice to go out with. Your friend tells you that he has arranged a blind date for you. Role-play the situation as you get all the important details.
5. You are a woman who has had a lovely evening with your date, but on the way to take you home, he suggests that you "go back to his place." Handle this situation tactfully by either agreeing or refusing. Remember that you wish to keep his friendship and his respect.
6. You are a man on a date with a young woman whom you don't know well. During the evening, you have held hands and kissed several times. At the end of the evening, she suggests that you "come back to her apartment." Handle this situation tactfully either by refusing or agreeing. Remember that you wish to keep her friendship and her respect.

4 | Summary

Read the situations described below and using the cultural information you have learned in this chapter try to figure out what the problem was and how it could have been avoided.

What's Going On Here? A. Read about the situation below, and then answer *Discussion Questions* with your classmates.

Peter, an international student who had recently arrived in the United States, liked a woman in one of his classes, but he didn't know how to get to know her. He thought she liked him, too, because whenever their eyes met, she smiled.

One night she phoned and asked him for a date. He was very surprised and said no. He said he was busy, although he really wasn't. What kind of girl was she to call him? No girls in his country would do that.

The next day in class Peter wouldn't look at her. She came over to him and said, "Hi. I'm sorry you can't go out with me on Saturday, but there's a big party on Friday. Would you like to go?" Peter said that he couldn't go, and then he rushed away. He didn't want anyone to see him talking to her because she obviously wasn't a nice girl. He wondered how he could ever have thought she was nice.

Discussion questions

1. Does Peter like her at first?
2. Why does he tell her he can't go out with her when she calls?
3. Why does he also say he can't go to the party?
4. He hurries away from her after the conversation. What do you think is the problem?
5. Why doesn't he think she is nice?

B. What is the cultural misunderstanding in the following situation? Answer the *Discussion Questions* in class after you have read about Timothy and Jennifer.

Timothy has recently arrived in Canada. He has a date on Saturday night with a Canadian girl named Jennifer; they plan to go out to dinner. He has seen many North American movies, and he knows that men sometimes take flowers to their dates. He doesn't have enough money to buy flowers, but he notices that there are some pretty yellow flowers growing on his front lawn. So he picks a huge handful of them and wraps them carefully in colored paper.

When Timothy arrives at Jennifer's house, he proudly hands her the flowers and says, "These are for you." She takes them and says, "Thank you for the dandelions," but he can tell from the look on her face that he has done something wrong.

Discussion questions

1. Why does Timothy bring flowers?
2. Where does he get the flowers?
3. What are dandelions? What kind of flower are they?
4. What kind of expression do you think Jennifer had on her face?

Speaking Out Consider each of these questions carefully, and then discuss your opinions with your classmates.

A. The disease AIDS has reached epidemic proportions in many countries. To limit discrimination against AIDS victims, the United States and Canada have passed laws which protect individuals with AIDS against job discrimination and make it illegal to reveal the fact that an individual has AIDS or has tested positive for the HIV virus.

1. Since AIDS is spread through sexual contact, should a person be required to reveal that he or she has AIDS or has tested positive for HIV before having sexual contact with another person? Why or why not? Should there be a penalty if a person does not inform his or her partner? What should the penalty be?
2. What do you think should be done to curb the spread of AIDS?

B. In the United States and Canada, premarital sex is common among high school and college students. Some people think that North American movies and television programs give the message that premarital sex is not only acceptable but desirable.

1. Using examples of programs and movies you have seen, explain why you agree or disagree with the statement above.
2. Ask several North American students if they agree that premarital sex is encouraged by the North American media. Compare their answers with yours.

C. "Date rape" occurs when a male forces his date to have sexual intercourse against her will during or after a date. Usually, the rape incident occurs at the college student's apartment, often after both have been drinking or indulging in passionate kissing and touching. Sometimes, the students have been on many dates and have had sexual intercourse before. In some cases, however, the students may be on a first date and the man forces himself on the woman who has done nothing to encourage his advances. There have been other incidents where the woman encourages the man to have intercourse with her and then says that he raped her, in order to get him into trouble.

1. When is the male responsible for date rape? What should the penalty be?
2. When is the female responsible for date rape? What should the penalty be?
3. What can you do to avoid being a victim of date rape? What advice would you give a person who is new to dating and unaware of what can happen in dating situations?

D. When you become involved in a serious relationship, your partner may ask you to tell about those you have dated and give details about your previous sexual relationships.

1. How much do you think you should tell? Why?
2. What would you want to know about the relationships a person you are in love with has had? Why?

E. Two proverbs relate to choosing a mate: "Opposites attract," and "Unless like marry like, there can be no happiness."

1. Which proverb do you agree with more? Why?
2. What things would you want to have in common with the person you marry?
3. What kinds of differences would you accept or prefer? Why?

F. It is not uncommon for men or women to visit the apartment of someone of the opposite sex unchaperoned in the United States or Canada. Often, a young woman will ask her date to her apartment for dinner or, after a date, to watch television or to have a snack. This does not mean that the woman is inviting her date to make advances toward her, nor, if a woman accepts an invitation to a man's apartment, does it mean that she wishes to have intimate relations with him.

1. How do you feel about people of the opposite sex visiting in each other's apartments without a chaperone?
2. Ask your North American friends how they feel about this. Discuss these opinions with the class.

G. North Americans are great matchmakers. They delight in "fixing someone up" with a date. The person is usually someone they know, who they believe would be compatible with the other person. As a person new to the United States or Canada, you may wish to ask your American friends to "fix you up" with a date so that you can get to know people of the opposite sex.

1. What questions should you ask your friend before you agree to go on a blind date?
2. What are your obligations to your blind date? Who pays for the date? What do you do if you wish to date the person again? What should you do if the date doesn't work out well?
3. Would you like to go on a blind date? Why or why not?

Five

Sharing Common Interests

International students are often surprised at North American attitudes toward humor, animals, and superstitions. For example, one student who was living with a North American family was shocked at how they treated the family dog. "I couldn't believe it," he said. "The dog had a bed in the child's room and was actually allowed to sit on the living room sofa. The dog even had his own food in cans, which is very expensive. Worse than that, they fed the dog right from the dining room table!"

North American humor also seems strange at times. For instance, North Americans enjoy making jokes about politicians and government policies. They even print bumper stickers that feature funny sayings about their attitudes and occupations, for example, "Nurses Are Patient People."

Although the United States and Canada are supposed to be very modern, they also have their share of superstitions, many of which are common to other cultures. Along with many other areas—such as gardening, sports, finance, and art—humor, superstition, and pets are common interests that are shared among friends.

1 North American Humor

Humor is universal; however, each culture finds different things funny. If you have evertried to translate a joke from your native language into another language, you probably were disappointed because your listener may not have thought it was funny. Something was, literally, "lost in the translation."

Try an experiment. Think of a joke that people in your culture find funny. Translate it into English, and write it on the lines below.

_____

_____

_____

_____

_____

_____

Now share your joke with someone from another culture. Does that person think it's funny?

Riddles   Like gestures, humor varies from one culture to another. In the United States and Canada, children often enjoy telling riddles. A riddle is a question that is hard to answer because it involves some kind of trick such as a play on words.

See if you can solve the following riddles. The answers are on page 180. After you check your answer, discuss the trick that made each riddle difficult to answer.

1. What has four wheels and flies? _____

2. What has four legs and no head? _____

3. What begins with *T*, ends with *T*, and has *T* in the middle? _____

4. What is black and white and "read" all over? _____

5. What would you have if you painted every automobile in the country pink? _____

Let's Share   Write a riddle that children in your country enjoy. Share it with the class.

_____

_____

_____

_____

Knock-Knock Jokes   Children also enjoy "knock-knock" jokes like these. One person pretends to be knocking at the door, and the other person pretends to answer.

ANN: Knock! Knock!

MARY: Who's there?

ANN: Ida

MARY: Ida who?

ANN: Ida Wanna. (*Ida Wanna* sounds like "I don't want to.")

***

TERESA: Knock! Knock!

MARTY: Who's there?

TERESA: Orange.

MARTY: Orange who?

TERESA: Orange you glad I'm your friend? (*Orange you* sounds like "aren't you.")

Notice that certain parts of the joke are always the same:

***

PHIL: *Knock! Knock!*

DON: *Who's there?*

PHIL: Boo.

DON: Boo *who?*

PHIL: Why are you crying?

Now You Do It   Try each of these jokes with a partner. Don't repeat the sentences in parentheses.

1. YOU: Knock! Knock!

   PARTNER: Who's there?

   YOU: Robert.

   PARTNER: Robert who?

   YOU: You mean you don't know either?

2. YOU: Knock! Knock!

   PARTNER: Who's there?

   YOU: Adam.

   PARTNER: Adam who?

   YOU: Adam up and give me the bill. (*Adam up* sounds like "add them up.")

3. YOU: Knock! Knock!

   PARTNER: Who's there?

   YOU: Sofa

   PARTNER: Sofa who?

   YOU: Sofa you're doing fine! (*sofa* sounds like "so far.")

4. Now try making up one of your own!

   YOU: Knock! Knock!

   PARTNER: Who's there?

   YOU: _____.

   PARTNER: _____.

   YOU: _____.

Analysis   North Americans value their ability to laugh at themselves and others. They enjoy jokes which make fun of professions such as doctors, lawyers, and politicians. Here are some examples of jokes. Try to figure them out before you read the explanations.

1. A doctor, a priest, and a lawyer found themselves stranded in the ocean. After their boat tipped over, a shark appeared and promptly ate the doctor and the

priest. Then he carried the lawyer on his back to safety. The lawyer was very surprised and asked the shark why he had killed the others but spared his life. The shark replied, "Professional courtesy."

Can you explain the meaning?

2. An American doctor told his patient that she needed surgery immediately. The cost of the operation was $12,000, but the patient could pay it off at the rate of $300 per month. "My goodness," replied the patient, "that's as much as buying a car!" "Yes," said the doctor, "I am."

Can you explain the meaning?

3. My son had the car out on Sunday and hit a tree. He insists it wasn't his fault because he blew the horn.

Can you explain the meaning?

Meanings

1. A shark is a dangerous, man-eating fish. Some people see lawyers who charge large fees for their services as being like sharks. "Professional courtesy" means people of the same or similar professions don't charge each other for their services.

2. The doctor is buying a new car and has set up his fees to cover his car payments. (This joke could be told in the United States but not in Canada.)

3. The stereotype of North American teenagers is that they think that they are always right. In this case, the teenager insists that the accident wasn't his fault because he blew the horn; the tree should have moved.

North Americans also enjoy humor that uses words with more than one meaning. Each of the words listed below has more than one meaning. Use a dictionary to find two different meanings for each word.

Word	First Meaning	Second Meaning
Patient		
Swingers		
Class		
Pull		
Kick		

Now look at the "one-liners" below. Can you explain their humor (double meanings)?

Nurses are patient people.
Tennis is for swingers.
Teachers have class.
Voters have pull.
Soccer players get a kick out of life.

Let's Share   Sayings like the ones just listed and the ones that follow are often found on T-shirts, bumper stickers, and buttons in the United States and Canada.

Saying	Meaning
Bald is beautiful.	Usually baldness is seen as negative. However, each person should be valued for who he is.
If you can read this, thank a teacher.	Teachers don't get enough recognition for the contribution they make.

What sayings do people in your country use? List them here with their meaning.

_____ .

_____ .

_____ .

Understanding North American Humor   The basis of humor is varied. Sometimes humor comes about unintentionally. For example, below are a number of responses that people wrote to explain to their insurance company how they got into an automobile accident. As you will see when you read them, the people who wrote these answers were very nervous. They were also trying to find a way not to blame themselves for causing the accident. The following quotes come from insurance forms and were published in the Toronto Sun, July 26, 1977.*

Read the quotes and discuss the questions that follow with your classmates.

Part 1

1. Coming home, I drove into the wrong house and collided with a tree I don't have.
2. The other car collided with mine without giving warning of its intentions.
3. I thought my window was down, but found it was up when I put my hand through it.
4. I collided with a stationary truck coming the other way.
5. A truck backed through my windshield into my wife's face.
6. A pedestrian hit me and went under my car.
7. The guy was all over the road; I had to swerve a number of times before I hit him.
8. I pulled away from the side of the road, glanced at my mother-in-law, and headed over the embankment.
9. In my attempt to kill a fly, I drove into a telephone pole.
10. I had been shopping for plants all day and was on my way home. As I reached an intersection, a hedge sprang up obscuring my vision. I did not see the other car.

*From "Understanding American Humor," *Toronto Sun,* July 26, 1977. Reprinted by permission of Press News Limited.

Discussion questions

1. Which ones are your favorites? Pick two and share them with your classmates. Why do you find them funny?
2. Which ones don't you understand?
3. Why are 2, 4 and 6 funny? What do they have in common?

Part 2

11. I had been driving my car for forty years when I fell asleep at the wheel and had an accident.
12. I was on my way to the doctor's with rear end trouble when my universal joint gave way causing me to have an accident.
13. As I approached the intersection, a stop sign appeared in a place where no stop sign had ever appeared before. I was unable to stop in time to avoid the accident.
14. To avoid hitting the bumper of the car in front, I struck the pedestrian.
15. My car was legally parked as it backed into the other vehicle.
16. An invisible car came out of nowhere, struck my vehicle and vanished.
17. I told the police that I was not injured but on removing my hat, I found that I had a skull fracture.
18. I was sure the old fellow would never make it to the other side of the road when I struck him.
19. The pedestrian had no idea which direction to go, so I ran over him.
20. I saw the slow-moving, sad-faced old gentleman as he bounced off the hood of my car.
21. The indirect cause of this accident was a little guy in a small car with a big mouth.
22. I was thrown from my car as it left the road. I was later found in a ditch by some stray cows.
23. The telephone pole was approaching fast. I was attempting to swerve out of its path when it struck my front end.
24. I was unable to stop in time, and my car crashed into the other vehicle. The driver and passenger then left immediately for a vacation with injuries.

Taken from the *Toronto Sun* July 26, 1977.

Discussion questions

1. Which three are your favorites? Why?
2. What is the joke in number 23?
3. In number 24, what is a "vacation with injuries"?
4. Who found the driver in number 22?
5. Why is number 19 funny?

Appreciating Humor   Sometimes when people don't know a language well, they make errors which are humorous. For example, there was a sign in a non-English-speaking country which read **Bargain basement one flight up.**

Anyone who knows English well knows that a "bargain basement" is a store where prices are low, but they also know that a basement is the area under a building and, therefore, can't be one flight up!

Below are some more signs which people have spotted in different parts of the world; they are funny because of their misuse of English.

1. *In a restaurant:*

    a. Special today: no ice cream.

b. The manager has personally passed all the water served here.

2. *In a dry cleaners or tailor shop:*

   a. Drop your trousers for best results.
   b. Ladies have fits upstairs.

3. *Detour sign on a highway:*
   Stop. Drive sideways.

4. *In a hotel:*
   Please leave your values at the desk.

5. *In a zoo:*
   Please do not feed the animals. If you have any suitable food, give it to the guard on duty.

(Information taken by permission from the *New Haven Register*, November 20, 1992; *TESL-L Bitnet*; Mike Kelley, the *Austin American Statesman* Aug. 9, 1990.)

Tongue Twisters

Many languages have sounds that are difficult to say, especially when the same or similar sound is repeated a number of times in succession. In English these sounds are called "tongue twisters." The trick, of course, is to learn to say them as fast as you can. They are also good for practicing pronunciation. How fast can you say these tongue twisters?

1. How much wood could a woodchuck chuck if a woodchuck could chuck wood?
2. She sells sea shells by the seashore.
3. Rubber baby buggy bumpers.
4. Peter Piper picked a peck of pickled peppers. If Peter Piper picked a peck of pickled peppers, how many peppers did Peter Piper pick?
5. The rain in Spain stays mainly on the plain.

2 Superstitions

Each culture has its own superstitions. Superstitions are beliefs that are not founded on scientific proof but nevertheless persist from generation to generation. Listed here are a number of superstitions people in North America may have.

Superstition	*Meaning*
Breaking a mirror	You will have seven years of bad luck.

Box continued on the following page

Box continued from the preceding page

Superstition	Meaning
Walking under a ladder	You will have bad luck.
Finding a four-leaf clover	You will have good luck.
A black cat's crossing your path	You will have bad luck.
The number 13	This is a very unlucky number. This superstition is so widely believed that many buildings do not have a 13th floor.
Knocking on wood	When you receive a compliment about yourself or a loved one or tell about something fortunate that has happened, you should "knock on wood" to prevent something bad from happening.
Crossing your fingers	You wish to have good luck.

Box continued on the following page

Box continued from the preceding page

Superstition	Meaning
Rabbit's foot	Carry it for good luck, although it didn't help the rabbit.
Horse shoe	Put it over the door of a new house to bring luck.

Matching: Superstitions

Match the statements in the first column with an appropriate response from the second column. Check your answers on page 180.

_____ 1. I have a physics exam and I need a score of 89 to get an *A* in the course.

_____ 2. We are in room 1313.

_____ 3. I haven't had a cold in three years.

_____ 4. I've had bad luck every year for the past six years.

_____ 5. Here's a shortcut. Let's go under this ladder.

_____ 6. I had a flat tire this morning; my boss said there would be no raises this year; my car is going to cost $1350 to fix.

A. That's bad luck.
B. Did you break a mirror?
C. I'll keep my fingers crossed.
D. That's double bad luck.
E. You'd better knock on wood.
F. Bad luck happens in threes.

Conversation Practice

After you have matched these statements with an appropriate response, practice the statements as part of conversations with a partner. Feel free to add additional comments if you wish.

Analysis

Different cultures have different ways of celebrating the New Year. In fact, in some countries around the world, the date of the New Year is not January 1 because the country uses a different calendar. For example, Israelis celebrate the New Year in the fall, and for Asians the New Year usually comes in February.

In North America the official New Year is January 1. However, people come to the United States and Canada from all over the world, and different populations may celebrate the New Year at different times and in different ways. Some people enjoy celebrating several of the different New Year's celebrations. North American Jews, for example, may celebrate Rosh Hashanah, the Jewish New Year, and join in the festivities on December 31 as well. Furthermore, they may go to a Chinese restaurant for the Chinese New Year and enjoy a very special and sumptuous Chinese meal. If they live in a big city with a large Chinese population, they may go to Chinatown to watch the dragon dancers.

How is the New Year celebrated in your country? Are there any rituals that people observe to keep away bad luck or to bring good luck? Share them with the class.

Read the following story, which describes how different ethnic groups in the United States celebrate the New Year. It tells how they hope to bring luck to themselves and their families and to ward off "evil spirits."

Happy New Year,
Now Go Eat Cabbage
By Maria Blackburn

Gannett News Service

So you want to celebrate the coming of the New Year.

First, gather your family around an open front door at midnight, then bang some pots and pans together and scream, "Horse s---, sailor, the sea's on fire!"

That's what Julie Routson's relatives in Fremont, Ohio, used to do.

Routson, now of Chesapeake, Va., says she "has no idea" where the custom came from. "It was something Aunt Doris started," she says.

Okay, so maybe you don't do this in your family.

But chances are you probably dust off the same set of New Year's traditions every year, even if you don't know where they came from or what they mean. On January 1, sometimes it's necessary to use a little folklore to ward off evil spirits and make sure the coming year is full of health, wealth and good luck.

Here are some examples of New Year's customs, and where they originated:

—Hog jaws, cabbage and black-eyed peas for New Year's dinner will bring luck. (North Carolina)

—If you cry on New Year's Day, you'll be sorry throughout the year. (Illinois)

—For New Year's, lobster represents good health and happiness. If in preparing it, the lobster is dropped or the feelers broken, a new lobster should be fixed. The feelers should be as symmetrical as possible. (Japanese-Americans living in Los Angeles)

—Always make sure your salt shaker is full on New Year's Day for good luck during the year. (The Ozarks)

—If people eat sauerkraut on New Year's Day they become rich. (Pennsylvania Dutch)

—Bad luck comes if a girl is your first visitor: good luck, if a man comes first. (Hawaii)

Even the experts don't know all the reasons behind these customs.

"There's many a story about how things started, but a lot of it is speculation, so no one can say for sure," says Janet Langlois, director of the Wayne State University Folklores Archive in Detroit, Mich.

Henry Grossi, a Washington, D.C. food historian, says the reason certain foods like pork, beans and cabbage are showcased in so many New Year celebrations is probably because before refrigeration existed, these foods had been preserved and were readily available during the winter.

"It could have been a matter of making a necessity into a virtue," says Grossi, whose mother's family from Croatia not only ate pork on New Year's, but also indulged in the tradition of "first-footing."

In this custom, people race to be the first person or "first foot" in the door of a neighbor's home. Alas, old world customs can be a bit sexist, and in Grossi's family, only males were rewarded with money for their efforts.

In some cases, the weirder the tradition, the longer it lingers in the family. Julie Routson's Aunt Doris died in 1975, but her plans for New Year's are the same as always. Come midnight, Routson and her family will be banging pots and pans on their front porch to herald the new year.

"It's just something you've got to do," she says.

From "Happy New Year, Now Go Eat Cabbage," by Maria Blackburn, *Democrat and Chronicle*, December 29, 1992. Reprinted by permission of Gannett News Service, Arlington, VA.

Let's Share   Do the following exercises with your class.

1. Divide into small groups and compile a list of superstitions common in your countries. One person from each group should be prepared to share that group's list with the class.

_____

_____

_____

_____

2. In North America, a holiday based on superstition is Halloween. This holiday originated with the belief that the souls of the dead, especially evil ones, walk the earth on October 31. On this day, children dress up in scary costumes and go from house to house shouting, "Trick or treat." People give children candy or prizes so that the children will not play a "trick," such as putting soap on their windows. Of course, most people no longer believe in evil spirits and witches but enjoy the holiday as a day of fun for children. Children should only go trick or treating in neighborhoods where they know the people. Candy or other food which is not in its original wrapper should be thrown away.

   Does your culture have a day that is surrounded by superstition? Tell your group or the class about this day and where the superstition came from.

3. Why do you think people are superstitious? Are people growing more or less superstitious? Why?

3   Telling "Ghost Stories"

North Americans are fascinated with the supernatural. They particularly like stories which tell about mysteries, spirits, and demons. These stories are often called "ghost stories." Here is a short story which takes place in a rural area of the United States. Please read it and answer the questions that follow.

The Underground People
By M.G. Law

"Boy, you stay away from that place, clean away," growled my Grandpa as he pointed a long, gnarled finger toward the abandoned house in the overgrown field below us.

"Why, Grandpa? Looks like just an old fallen down house to me," I said, peering through the trees. In those days, I thought I had to know everything. Now I know I don't.

He hesitated for a long moment and looked away. Then with a sigh of resignation, he said, "Nobody's ever had any luck there. Never. Not from the day the place was built. Just one bad thing after another 'til folks just packed up and let the place fall to pieces. Those who didn't, should have."

"What happened, Grandpa?" I asked expectantly.

"Well, about 1930, a young couple built their house out there. Things went fine for them at first, until the wife began to hear crying, and mumbling under the floor. She ignored it at first—said it was the wind or trees brushing against the house.

"Then the voices started telling her things, dark things. They whispered and growled and shuffled under the floor boards, but only she could hear them. No one, not even her husband, believed that they were there.

"As time went by, the voices, which she called the underground people, got louder and more threatening. They tried to lure her to kill her family, to come down below with them forever, but she resisted.

"First, she tried to set fires on the floor of her house to drive them away. Her husband saw the smoke just in time to get back and put out the flames. He found her in her rocking chair with their child in her arms while she watched the fire burn. She was streaked with soot, laughing and crying hysterically. After that, he sent her back East to stay with her family for a while.

"A year later, she came back, but it started all over again. She got worse and worse until finally, her husband caught her chopping up the kitchen floor. She screamed over and over again that they were chopping through the kitchen floor from below to get her. After that, he put her in the Institute for crazy people over in DeWitt County.

"The fellow moved out the next week and never came back. Folks tried to live in the place after that but they never had any luck. Seems they always had the urge to move on fairly quickly. No one goes near it—no one but a fool would."

With that, he gave me a stern, deep look and began to move swiftly down the trail. Obviously, the subject was closed as far as he was concerned.

But the subject wasn't closed as far as I was concerned. All I could think of was that house, the voices, and the ax marks on the floor. It was almost as if the house were calling me, saying, "Come here, boy, and find out for yourself."

Well, I did. One evening after I had finished chores, I sneaked back to the house, armed with a flashlight and our old hunting dog. The old house shimmered and wove in the summer twilight, mesmerizing me and drawing me in, although the dog flatly refused to go another foot.

Simultaneously repelled and drawn, I cautiously opened the kitchen door and stepped in. A gentle breeze wafted the thick cobwebs that draped over the walls and her rocking chair that stood beside the old, grimy wood cookstove. The smells of loss and failure mixed with the dark, earthy odor rising from the jagged hole in the middle of the floor. A single china cup lay broken in the sink.

Then I heard it—voices, not loud or clear but wheedling, whispering, luring. From the corner of my eye, I saw the rocking chair moving rhythmically to the tune of a gentle lullaby. I wanted to run, but couldn't. They were calling my name.

Dropping to my knees, I put my ear to the floor. I could hear chopping and the splintering of wood. I crept slowly toward the hole in the floor. I had to know.

Shining my light into the hole, I got my answer. There were ax marks in the boards all right, but the cuts had been made from below.

I got out of there as fast as I could, and I never intend to go back. No, I won't tell you where the place is because no one but a fool would go there.

Discussion questions

1. What did the grandfather say happened in the abandoned house?
2. Why did the grandfather hesitate to tell the story?
3. Why did the young man go to the abandoned house even though his grandfather told him not to go? Was he wrong to go there?
4. What happened to the young man when he went to the house?
5. Why won't the young man tell where the house is? Would you go to the house if you knew how to get there? Why or why not?
6. The writer tells this as a true story. Do you believe things like this happen? Why? Share your reasons.
7. Can you think of a ghost story to share with your class? Divide into small groups and tell ghost stories.

Exploring North America

In this exercise you will have an opportunity to find out more about North American culture.

1. Ask a North American friend to tell you his or her favorite ghost story. Share the story with your class.
2. Many North American movies deal with the supernatural. Visit a video store or review the movie listing in your local newspaper; then write down the names of three movies and a sentence telling what each is about.

3. Ask your North American friends to tell you some of their superstitions. Then ask them if they believe in the superstitions on pages 76–78. Discuss their answers with the class.
4. Ask your North American friends why frightening movies like *Friday the 13th* are so popular. Discuss their answers with the class.

Speaking Out

Read about the American holiday of Halloween and discuss the issue of going trick or treating.

In years past, Halloween was a light-hearted holiday in which children wearing costumes went from house to house in their neighborhoods to collect "treats." Treats were usually a cookie, an apple, or a small piece of candy. If they weren't given a treat, children sometimes put soap on people's windows or rang their doorbells and ran away. Now, because some people have tried to hurt children, many parents no longer let their children go out to trick-or-treat. Instead, they have Halloween parties for their children at home or insist that they go only to the homes of people they know.

Some people think that not allowing children to trick-or-treat is a good thing because they resented having to give out treats and having children play tricks on them. Others think that children are missing an important part of growing up. How do you feel about the tradition of trick or treat?

4 | Attitudes Toward Wild Animals and Pets

Many North Americans have pets. Pets can be dogs or cats, gerbils, hamsters, mice, guinea pigs, parakeets, canaries, or tropical fish. Pets usually live in the house and are treated with great care and affection. Dogs and cats generally have the freedom to walk around in the house, and their food is usually kept on the floor in the kitchen. It is not unusual for pets to be fed from the family table.

Here is a list of facts about pets in North America.

1. North Americans spend a great deal of money on their pets every year. Some even buy coats and fancy collars for their dogs and cats.
2. It is against the law in North America to mistreat an animal. A person might have to pay a large fine or even go to jail if convicted.
3. The cost of pet care is so high that insurance companies are beginning to sell health insurance for pets.
4. People sometimes bury their pets in very expensive pet cemeteries. These cemeteries sometimes allow the owner to be buried beside the pet, just as parents and children are buried near each other in other cemeteries. Sometimes people buy large, stone headstones for their pet's grave.
5. Some dogs and cats are fed directly from the table and are given beds and pillows in the house. They are treated "like one of the family."

Choose one of the statements on this list. After you have carefully organized your thoughts, tell your classmates what you think about the information in the statement. Then tell how people in your country treat pets.

Exploring North America

Read the information below, find out as much as you can about the subject and discuss the cultural issues.

1. Many advertisements feature either animated or real animals to advertise products. Describe two of these advertisements appearing on Canadian or American television or in magazine advertisements. Ask your North American friends if these advertisements appeal to them and why. Share their reasons with the class. Do these advertisements appeal to you? Why or why not?
2. Find out if there is a Humane Society or a Society for the Prevention of Cruelty to Animals (SPCA) in your community. Report to the class about what it does and how. What does the existence of these organizations tell you about North American attitudes toward animals?

3. Visit a local pet store or the pet section of a large department store. List the types of toys, clothing, bedding, and accessories that people can purchase for their pets. Ask your North American friends what they would need to buy if they had a dog or cat. What would you buy? What wouldn't you buy? Why?

4. Studies have shown that having a pet has a positive effect on the owner's mental health. For example, watching fish in an aquarium can help lower a person's blood pressure. Pets are brought to nursing homes to give the older residents something to love and to touch. This helps these individuals feel physically and mentally better because it gives them an outlet for their love as well as an interest. Ask your North American friends how they feel about their pets and why they have them. Do you believe that a pet can have a positive effect on someone? Why?

What's Going On Here?

Read about Emily's visit to the Morgans. Then, with your classmates, answer the questions that follow.

When Emily had been in the United States for only a week, she was invited to the home of an American family. She was very excited about seeing the inside of an American house; she knew that most tourists never got inside a real home.

Mrs. Morgan picked her up at her hotel, and they headed out on the highway to Mrs. Morgan's home. She had met Mrs. Morgan two days before, and she liked her very much.

After about a 15-minute drive, they entered an area with big lawns and lovely houses. Emily told Mrs. Morgan that it looked beautiful.

Soon they turned into a driveway, and there in front of them was a beautiful white house—with pillars! There were lots of trees and flowers around the front yard.

Two boys, aged 10 and 12, came running up to the car with a big brown dog. Mrs. Morgan introduced them as her sons, Greg and Todd. The dog she said was Rover.

They went into the house, and Rover disappeared into the kitchen. She could hear him lapping up water. Soon they sat down to have lunch. Mrs. Morgan had cold cuts, a salad, and cookies on the table; they each made themselves a sandwich.

Rover sat under the table, and Greg kept bending down and giving him food to eat. Mrs. Morgan told him to stop doing it.

Emily couldn't eat everything, and as Todd helped his mother clear the table, he took Emily's plate and put it on the floor. Immediately, Rover came over and ate the rest of Emily's sandwich. Todd picked up the plate and brought it into the kitchen.

Suddenly, Emily felt nauseated. She wanted to run out of this dirty, disgusting house. Mrs. Morgan had seemed so nice and clean. But now she realized she wasn't. How Emily wished that she had never come to their house and that she had never eaten that sandwich.

Discussion questions

1. How long had Emily been in the United States?
2. Why was she excited about going to Mrs. Morgan's house?
3. Who did she meet at the house?
4. What did they eat for lunch?
5. Where was the dog while they ate?
6. Did Emily finish eating her sandwich?
7. What did Todd do after the meal?
8. Why was Emily so upset?

Among the controversial issues North Americans are talking about is how to protect the environment. Everyone wants to ensure clean air and water and to protect the earth's many species of plants and animals, but at what cost? There is controversy about what steps to take. Some people are concerned that measures taken to protect the environment and endangered or threatened species will result in an unacceptable number of jobs lost. Others are concerned that protecting certain plants and animals will slow down the technological progress they consider more important.

The following article, "Should These Five Survive?" by Michael Tennesen, describes five species that are threatened or endangered. Read the article, and then discuss with your classmates the claims made by each side in the endangered-species debate.

Should these five survive?
By Michael Tennesen

Every year, experts struggle with the debate over dollars vs. hundreds of dwindling species. This year, they must decide.

The Endangered Species Act protects more than 600 species of plants and animals, limiting development in their habitats and providing money for research and preservation. The act, first passed in 1973, is up for renewal this year. Congress began preliminary talks in late March; action is not expected until late spring. Supporters say the act is needed more than ever as more species are threatened with extinction. Critics say the act doesn't consider human costs: loss of jobs and a weakened economy. Here's a look at five endangered or threatened species.

Sea Turtle: At Loggerheads With Economics

Every year, female loggerhead sea turtles lay up to 100 eggs each in prime nesting sites on Florida's East Coast. Usually only one in 10,000 hatchlings survive to adulthood. The species is listed as "threatened." The debate: The act limits shore development in nesting areas and requires "turtle excluder" devices on shrimp nets.

Shrimpers report losing up to 25 percent of their catch (government estimates are closer to 7 percent). If the act doesn't pass: State law still would protect nesting sites, but unmodified nets could kill 55,000 loggerheads a year, moving the turtle to "endangered" status.

Grizzly Bear: Confined to Alaska?

Grizzlies in the lower 48 states live in six locales, mostly in Montana and Wyoming's Yellowstone National Park. But grizzlies need lots of space. The debate: Preserving grizzly habitat under the act often means shutting off commercial access. In northeastern Montana, for instance, loggers can't cut timber in 30 to 40 percent of the local national forest land—mostly to protect the bear's territory. "That's like looking down a block of 10 families and saying, OK now, three or four of you are

out of work," says Bruce Vincent, of Communities for a Great Northwest in Libby, Mont. If the act doesn't pass: Grizzlies might disappear except in Alaskan wilderness areas.

The Peregrine Falcon: Flying Back

This regal predator almost was wiped out in the '50s and '60s. The culprit? The pesticide DDT. Thanks to a DDT ban and efforts to place aviary-hatched falcons in the wild, 890 breeding pairs now fly high across the USA—even from skyscraper

perches in Baltimore, Los Angeles and New York. The debate: Some say the falcon should come off the endangered species list, since it has bounded back. But others say the numbers are still too small, especially if the bird is no longer protected by the act.

Carolina Northern Flying Squirrel: Vanishing Into Thin Air?

This nocturnal glider is limited to eight isolated mountaintops in North Carolina and Tennessee. The debate: Is the squirrel worth trying to save? Humans aren't the obvious threat; there's little development in its habitat. Its disappearance could be the

natural selection process at work. If the act doesn't pass: Research funds would dry up, and scientists may never learn why the squirrel is dying out—or if it should have been saved.

Snake River Sockeye Salmon: Upstream Battle

Last year, only four sockeyes survived the trip up 900 miles of rivers and past eight major dams from the Pacific Ocean to their sole spawning grounds in Idaho. The debate: Rebuilding dams so salmon could get by could cost $300 million and increase utility costs 4 to 8 percent—a heavy blow to agricultural irrigators. "People

are more important than fish," says Rayola Jacobsen, of the Idaho Farm Bureau. If the act doesn't pass: The Snake River sockeye salmon may die out, as may other species of salmon and steelhead. Says salmon specialist Ed Chaney: "They'd kill them all. It would be a done deal."

From "Should These Five Survive?," by Michael Tennesen. *USA Weekend*, April 17–19, 1992. Reprinted by permission of the author.

6 Health

Many North Americans are paying more attention to improving their health.

Diet Because of an increase in heart disease in North America, Canadians and Americans have become increasingly conscious of their health. They try to follow low-cholesterol and low-sodium diets. As a result, many have switched from a diet heavy in red meat to a diet in which they eat more grains, fruits, and vegetables. People tend to eat more fish and chicken now instead of beef. Some have become vegetarians.

In the chart below, compare the typical North American diet of the past with the diets North Americans try to follow now, then fill in the last column to indicate how people eat in your country and culture. Be prepared to explain if it is different or the same as it was 20 years ago.

Let's Share

North American Meals	Old-fashioned Diet	Current Diet	Diet in Your Country/Culture
Breakfast	orange juice 2 eggs (fried) or scrambled) toast and butter bacon or sausage coffee or tea	orange juice cereal (hot or cold) or toast and margarine coffee or tea	
Lunch	hamburger and french fries or a sandwich beverage	salad or a sandwich beverage (often mineral water)	
Dinner	steak or fried chicken mashed potatoes food prepared in cream sauces cake, pie, or ice cream beverage	broiled chicken (without the skin) fresh vegetables (steamed) fresh fruit beverage	

More North Americans prepare food now by broiling it or baking it, and they eat less fried food. How is food prepared in your country? What is people's attitude toward food in your country? Do they worry about eating too much red meat? Do they eat food with a lot of cream sauces? Do they eat a lot of fresh fruits and vegetables? Fish? Grains such as beans, or rice?

Exercise In addition to changes in diet, North Americans have discovered the importance of exercise. They may belong to health clubs where they do aerobic exercise and work out on exercise equipment in the gym; they may jog or have exercise equipment at home which they try to use three or four times a week. Some people buy exercise videotapes which they use to work out at home.

Do people get a lot of exercise in your country? What is their attitude toward exercise?

Smoking   More and more North Americans are aware of the dangers associated with cigarette smoking. Every package of cigarettes purchased in the United States or in Canada has words similar to these written on it: WARNING: THE SURGEON GENERAL HAS DETERMINED THAT CIGARETTE SMOKING IS DANGEROUS TO YOUR HEALTH.

In addition, cigarettes may not be advertised on television, and individuals must be 18 years old to purchase them. Unfortunately, this is hard to enforce since cigarettes can be purchased from vending machines.

Smoking is not permitted on domestic flights in the United States or in Canada. Public places such as airports, restaurants, places of business, and so forth do not allow smoking either. They might have a smoking and a nonsmoking section or area. If you wish to smoke, you must make sure you're in a smoking area before you light up.

When you go to a restaurant, check with the other people in your party to see if they prefer a smoking or nonsmoking section. Then tell the host which you prefer so you can be seated in the appropriate section.

When you go to someone's home, check to see if there are ashtrays set out on tables. If there aren't, that probably means the people you are visiting do not smoke. In that case, you should not light up. If you need to smoke, excuse yourself and go outside, or ask if there is a place where you can have a cigarette.

What is the attitude toward smoking in your country? Are there any policies regulating smoking? Do many people smoke? Are smokers trying to quit?

Drinking

Canada is made up of provinces. Provincial governments have jurisdiction over certain areas within their province. Provincial governments can collect taxes and make laws regarding education, housing, and the drinking age.

The United States is a confederation of states. States have the right to make laws with regard to their state so long as the federal government doesn't have jurisdiction in that area. For example, states determine policies regarding education, and they may collect a state income tax; they also determine the speed limit, housing codes, and the drinking age.

In most parts of North America, you must be 21 years old to buy alcohol in a liquor store, bar, or restaurant. In some U.S. states you may buy beer or wine in a grocery store. If a store sells alcohol to a minor, the owner of the store is usually fined.

In addition, many areas have an open-container law, which means that people may not drink alcohol on the street or in a car. Anyone caught with an open container of alcohol may be arrested.

Nevertheless, with all of these laws, the consumption of alcohol is a serious problem in the United States and Canada. Drinking on college campuses, where there are many underage drinkers, has increased greatly. In fact, alcohol consumption has increased since the legal drinking age was changed from 18 to 21. Some people believe that if there were no drinking age, as in some other countries, North American youth would drink less.

Others feel that enforcement of the law should be stricter. In the meantime, many automobile accidents are caused by people who drink and drive. (The offense is called *DWI*, driving while intoxicated.) There is also an increase in date rape, which many attribute to alcohol.

What is the drinking policy in your country? When do people begin to drink? What is the law? Do you think young people drink less when there is no legal drinking age?

What's Going On Here?

What cultural misunderstanding took place at Marion's house? Read about the following situation, and discuss the questions below.

Marion was very angry after Jeff left her house. She had met him in her biology class, and when she learned he was new in the United States, she invited him to come to her house for dinner. Her mother prepared a special meal and was looking forward to meeting this young man who had traveled halfway around the world to study in the United States. So how could Jeff have been so rude?

No sooner did he come into the house than he took out a cigarette and asked if anyone else would like one. Marion's mother said as politely as she could, "Oh, uh, sorry we don't smoke." But Jeff didn't take the hint. Couldn't he see that there were no ashtrays anywhere? He lit his cigarette anyway and put the ashes in the candy dish!

When the smoke blew in her face, Marion's mother even coughed and waved the smoke away. It's true that Jeff then put the cigarette behind his back, but why hadn't he just put it out.

The dinner was a disaster. All that good food and all that terrible smoke. Jeff must have had five cigarettes in three hours! Marion couldn't wait for him to leave. And when he did, she and her mother immediately opened all the windows.

Marion's mother said, "We'll have to wash our clothes to get the smell out. What a rude young man. Even after I told him we didn't smoke, he went right on smoking. I even waved the smoke out of my face and he didn't stop. How rude! We won't invite **him** again."

Discussion questions

1. Did Jeff know that he was being rude?

2. How did Marion's mother let Jeff know that she didn't want him to smoke? What three things should have told Jeff not to smoke in their house?
3. Why did Jeff ignore this information?
4. How might the bad feelings in this encounter have been prevented or remedied?

7   Music

North Americans are great music lovers. Twenty-four hours a day, you can listen to every type of music on the radio in the United States. If you have cable television, you can watch MTV, which shows videos of popular songs, or watch public television, which carries concerts of great orchestras from around the world. You can even attend the symphony or go to a rock concert, depending on the type of music you prefer.

Exploring North America

A. For each type of music listed on the chart below, write a definition and an example. Get the information from a friend, or look it up in a dictionary. Then answer the questions that follow.

Type of Music	Definition	Example
Rock and roll		
Heavy metal		
Country and Western		
Easy listening		

Box continued on the following page

Box continued from the preceding page

Type of Music	Definition	Example
Gospel		
Rap		
Soul		

Who are the most popular recording artists in North America? What are the ten most popular rock and roll songs this week? Ask your North American friends, consult the "Top Ten" listing in your local newspaper, or call a local radio station and ask.

From what you observe, what must a singer or group do or be to become popular in North America?

Speaking Out   Be prepared to discuss the issues presented.

A. MTV (Music-Television) is a 24-hour cable television channel which features videos of popular songs. Young people are the primary audience for this channel. The videos are designed to create an image of the song that the viewers will re-create in their minds when they hear the song played on the radio.

Some people object to the videos because they think that these images block the imagination of the viewers and keep them from forming and enjoying their own image of the song. Do you agree with that criticism? Why or why not?

B. The lyrics of North American songs have become increasingly violent and sexual over the past 20 years. For example, before the 60s, popular songs had no profanity or direct sexual references. Various groups in the United States have tried to ban songs with obscene lyrics or satanic content. Various singing groups have said that the Constitution of the United States gives them freedom of speech and that to deny them the chance to say and sing what they want violates their rights. Do you agree with these groups? Why or why not?

Six

Participating in Social Events

Religious customs and social events are central to any culture. They provide the means to deal with birth, marriage, and death. These events are also the stepping-stones to adulthood and acceptance in the community. In this chapter, we will discuss various social events, ways to deal with difficult social situations, and conversations appropriate to each. As you work through this chapter, be sure to apply what you have learned and discussed in earlier chapters so that you can sharpen your speaking skills and gain a deeper understanding of North American culture.

Photo Essay Can you tell what is happening in the photographs on page 95 and 96? What function is taking place? Find the answers on the bottom of page 96.

A

B

C

Photo identifications: (A) a child's birthday party; (B) a wedding; (C) a funeral.

1 Social Events

Let's Share Here is a chart of important social events and ways that they are observed in the United States and Canada. After you discuss these North American customs with your class, write how you observe these occasions in your culture.

Event	Observance in the United States or Canada	Observance in Your Country
Birth	Friends give a baby shower for expectant mother; people send gifts for baby, flowers for the mother in the hospital; and send birth announcement to friends; people send greeting cards to new parents.	
Birthday	Adults celebrate with family and usually have a cake with candles; children have parties, invite friends, wear hats, play games, receive prizes, eat cake and ice cream; guests bring relatively inexpensive presents.	
Marriage	*Engagement:* Fiancé gives his future wife a ring, usually with a diamond; the bride's friends give bridal showers, where the bride receives household gifts; friends of the groom give him a "stag party." *Wedding:* Guests attend the ceremony and, if invited, a reception afterwards; guests give gifts, usually of expensive silver, china, or glassware, or they give money.	
Wedding anniversary	Husband and wife spend the evening together or go out with friends. On the 25th and 50th wedding anniversary, family and friends give the couple a special party and bring them presents.	

Box continued on the following page

Box continued from the preceding page

Event	Observance in the United States or Canada	Observance in Your Country
Death	*Funeral home:* Friends gather at the funeral home or chapel to pay their respects, offer condolences; they send flowers or make a contribution to a charity in the name of the deceased. *Funeral:* Family and close friends go to the religious service and then to the cemetery to pay their respects.	

Analysis   After examining the pictures at the beginning of this chapter, fill in the chart below, describing the type of clothing worn at each event. Then fill in the part of the chart describing the clothes worn in your country. When you have finished, share this information with your classmates.

Event	Dress in the United States or Canada	Dress in Your Country
Birthday party for children		
Wedding ceremony		
Funeral		

Saying the Right Thing at Weddings and Funerals

2

Conversationally and emotionally, weddings and funerals are two of the most difficult events to attend. Although weddings are festive, happy times, guests often know few people and therefore must have sharp conversational skills, especially for small talk. Funerals are even more difficult because you want to say something consoling to the family of the deceased but often cannot find the words. This section provides a guide for conversation at these events; you can shape the language to your own needs and feelings.

Attending a Wedding: Appropriate Conversation

Weddings are festive times. The two families plan the wedding and reception together, although the bride's family generally pays for the wedding. Usually the bride wears a long white gown and veil to signify purity, and the groom and his attendants wear tuxedos. Guests generally wear dressy clothes to the service and reception.

The reception is a party for the bride and groom after the wedding service; to attend the reception, you must be invited. At the reception, there is a receiving line made up of the bride and groom and their families. Guests pass from person to person in the receiving line to give their congratulations and good wishes. Gifts are either sent to the bride's house before the wedding or brought to the reception.

Small talk, as you learned in chapter 2, is light conversation about general subjects such as the weather. Small talk is particularly useful when you don't know the other person well and wish to begin a conversation. This type of conversation usually lasts only a few minutes. Here are some of the types of small talk people engage in at different times at a wedding.

Model Dialogues

Here are examples of conversations that might take place at a wedding reception.

1. YOU: What a handsome couple they make.

   ACQUAINTANCE: Yes, isn't she a lovely bride!

   YOU: Do you know where they plan to honeymoon?

   ACQUAINTANCE: Yes. I believe they're going to Niagara Falls.

   YOU: That's a popular honeymoon spot in North America, isn't it?

   ACQUAINTANCE: Yes. Where are you from?

   YOU: I'm from Nigeria.

   ACQUAINTANCE: Where do people in your country honeymoon?

2. ACQUAINTANCE: Which side of the family are you with?

   YOU: I'm a friend of the bride's.

   ACQUAINTANCE: Oh. I'm the groom's uncle, Jim Martin.

   YOU: Nice to meet you. I'm Barbara Fields.

   ACQUAINTANCE: How do you know the bride?

   YOU: We went to high school together.

Attending a Funeral: Appropriate Conversation

In the United States and Canada, people belong to many religions. Most people, however, are Catholic, Protestant, or Jewish. Each handles death in a different way. In the Protestant and Catholic religions, religious services are held at a church; in the Jewish religion, at a synagogue. In addition to attending the religious service, people may go to a funeral home to express their sympathy to a grieving family. In the Jewish religion, people may go to the funeral home to express sympathy and may also pay a visit to the grieving family during the next week. At this time, the family is "sitting shiva" at the home of one of its members. People who come to pay their respects may bring candy or fruit.

When attending a funeral, you should wear simple clothing of either dark or neutral shades. In some parts of North America and among Jews, it is customary to return to the house of the deceased for a light lunch if you are a close friend of the family. The food is provided by friends of the family and may be anything from desserts to a full meal, including a meat dish.

Although most North Americans send flowers, they also make contributions to charities in the deceased's name, especially if requested by the family to do so instead of sending flowers. The obituary notice in the newspaper will state the charity to which the family wishes the donations to be sent.

Model Dialogues

Here are some samples of conversations you might hear to express sympathy.

1. YOU: He (she) certainly was a wonderful person.

   BEREAVED PERSON: Yes. We'll miss him (her) very much.

2. BEREAVED PERSON: I just spoke to him (her) last week.

   YOU: He (she) was very special to me. I remember when . . . (*tell incident*)

3. YOU: I'm sorry about your loss.

   BEREAVED PERSON: I will miss him (her) so much.

   YOU: I know. It's a very sad time.

Sometimes we don't know people well enough to attend the funeral but still wish to express sympathy.

4. YOU: I was sorry to hear about your (mother, father, sister, brother, husband, wife, child, friend).

   FRIEND: Thank you.

Now You Do It

Now it's your turn!

1. In groups of three, take turns role-playing these situations. Make sure that you use appropriate body language and gestures. The person who is watching the role-play should evaluate how the other two students handle each situation.

   a. Tell the mother of the bride how lovely her daughter looks and that you wish the couple happiness.
   b. You meet a friend at a wedding and talk about the bride or groom. You may talk about where she or he lives or goes to school, how long they have known each other, where they met, and so forth.
   c. Your close friend has died. Express your sympathy to your friend's brother or sister.
   d. Your teacher's father, whom you didn't know, has died. Express your sympathy to your teacher.

2. Be prepared to discuss with your class how funeral and wedding customs are different in your country. Choose one event from either a wedding or funeral and discuss its significance.

3 Celebrating Holidays and Special Events

Holidays often represent religious or patriotic events that most of the people in a country share in celebrating. In many countries, there is a state religion. The government and the religious leaders may work together to set political policies and decide on government actions.

In the United States, however, people believe in the separation of church and state. This means that the government may not interfere with or support matters relating to religion, and religious institutions may not interfere in matters of government.

Because people living in the United States and Canada come from all over the world, they have learned to enjoy holidays that are part of other people's cultures but not their own and to respect people's right to worship in their own way. For example, most Americans, Christian or not, enjoy attending Christmas parties. They may also wear the customary green on St. Patrick's Day even though they are not Irish.

North American Holidays

Here is a list of North American holidays, when they are celebrated, and some information about how they are celebrated.

Holiday	Time of Year	Type of Celebration
New Year's Eve	Evening of December 31	People dress up to go out to dinner, movies, theater, or parties. Most parties begin at 9:00 or 10:00 P.M.
New Year's Day	January 1	People relax from the previous evening's festivities. They may visit with friends. Many watch college football on television.

101

Box continued from the preceding page

Holiday	Time of Year	Type of Celebration
Martin Luther King Jr.'s Birthday (U.S.)	January 15	Some schools and businesses close in honor of this slain civil rights leader.
Valentine's Day	February 14	Children exchange greeting cards in school. Sweethearts exchange cards. Men give flowers or candy to the women they love (wife, daughter, mother, girlfriend). Women may give gifts, too.
Presidents' Day (combined celebration of Washington's Birthday and Lincoln's Birthday) (U.S.)	Third Monday in February	Many schools close for a week's vacation. Banks and the post office close for the day.
St. Patrick's Day	March 17	This is an Irish holiday, celebrated with parades. People wear green.

Box continued on the following page

Box continued from the preceding page

Holiday	Time of Year	Type of Celebration
April Fools' Day	April 1	This is a day when people, especially children, like to play tricks on others.
Passover	Eight days in the spring	This Jewish religious holiday celebrates the Jews' escape from slavery in Egypt. On the first two nights, Jewish people have a traditional family meal called a *seder*.
Easter	A Sunday in the U.S. and Canada in the spring (March-April)	This is a Christian religious holiday. Some people stay home from work or school on the preceding Friday (Good Friday). On Easter Sunday, Christian families attend church and gather for traditional meals. (In addition, many North Americans enjoy buying chocolate Easter bunnies, candy eggs, and jelly beans. There are Easter egg hunts, and children color Easter eggs.)
Mother's Day	Second Sunday in May	The extended family gathers; mothers and grandmothers receive cards and gifts.

Box continued on the following page

Box continued from the preceding page

Holiday	Time of Year	Type of Celebration
Victoria Day (Canada)	Third Monday in May	Named after Queen Victoria, this holiday celebrates the birthday of the monarch under whose reign Canada became a dominion (in 1867).
Memorial Day (U.S.)	Last Monday in May	This day honors all who have died in war. Schools and all government offices and businesses are closed.
Father's Day	Third Sunday in June	Families gather; fathers and grandfathers receive cards and gifts.
St. Jean Baptiste Day (Quebec, Canada)	June 24	This holiday celebrates Quebec's patron saint with big fanfare. Everything is closed, and there are parties on Mount Royale, open air concerts, parades, and street parties.

Box continued on the following page

Box continued from the preceding page

Holiday	Time of Year	Type of Celebration
Canada Day (Canada)	July 1	Formerly called Dominion Day, this holiday acknowledges Canada as a country. It is a major holiday, celebrated with fireworks and parties.
Independence Day (U.S.)	July 4	The day the American colonies declared independence from England is celebrated with parades, picnics, barbecues, and fireworks.
Civic Holiday (Ontario, Canada)	First Monday in August	This is a holiday celebrated in the province of Ontario.
Labor Day	First Monday in September	This is usually the final summer vacation before school begins. People go on picnics and have outdoor parties with family and friends. A holiday commemorating the efforts of working people.

Box continued on the following page

Box continued from the preceding page

Holiday	Time of Year	Type of Celebration
Rosh Hashanah	Two days in the fall	This is the Jewish New Year, celebrated by going to synagogue.
Yom Kippur	Tenth day following Rosh Hashanah	This is the Day of Atonement in the Jewish religion; Jews fast and go to synagogue.
Columbus Day (U.S)	October 12	This holiday celebrates the day Christopher Columbus discovered America. Schools, banks, and post offices are closed.
Thanksgiving Day (Canada)	Second Monday in October	This holiday commemorates the last harvest of the year. People have a day off from work.

Box continued on the following page

Box continued from the preceding page

Holiday	Time of Year	Type of Celebration
Halloween	October 31	Children dress up in costumes and go door to door saying "trick or treat." They expect people to give them candy or other treats.
Veterans' Day (U.S.)	November 11	This is a day honoring all people who have served in the armed forces; people display flags, and there are parades.
Remembrance Day (Canada)	November 11	This day honors those who died defending their country in war. Government offices closed; offices are closed; schools and stores are open. At 11:00 A.M. students stand for a moment of silence.
Thanksgiving (U.S.)	Fourth Thursday in November	This holiday commemorates the Pilgrims' first harvest in the New World. It is celebrated with a large meal, traditionally including roast turkey.

Box continued on the following page

Box continued from the preceding page

Holiday	Time of Year	Type of Celebration
Hanukkah	Eight days in late fall	This is the Jewish Festival of Lights; families light candles and exchange small gifts on each of the eight nights.
Christmas Day	December 25	This is the Christian holiday celebrating the birth of Jesus Christ. Families gather to exchange gifts and eat a traditional meal. Families decorate Christmas trees with ornaments and sing songs. Santa Claus, a fat, jolly man in a white beard, brings gifts to all.
Boxing Day (Canada)	December 26	This is a holiday celebrated the day after Christmas. The stores are open and offer the biggest sales of the year.

Look at the photos and see if you can identify the holidays. Refer to the chart if necessary. Check your answers on page 180.

1.

2.

3.

4.

5.

Greeting Cards Sending greeting cards is a popular way for North Americans to express their feelings on a variety of occasions. Cards are printed not only for birthdays and anniversaries, Mother's Day and Father's Day, Christmas and New Year's, but also for graduation, Valentine's Day, and many other events. People in the United States and Canada send get-well cards to people who are ill, and they even send cards to express friendship. However, with the exception of Christmas (Season's Greetings/New Year's) cards, you should know people well or see them often before sending them a card or buying them a gift. The only time it is appropriate to give a gift to someone you don't know well is if you are invited to a party to celebrate a birthday or an anniversary. Some business-people send cards to clients to maintain goodwill. Some people rarely send cards.

Matching: Greeting Cards

For what occasion would you buy the following greeting cards? Match the message inside the card with the event. Check your answers on page 180.

Message

_____ 1. Sorry to hear of your loss.

_____ 2. Another year, another gray hair.

_____ 3. May the bells always be ringing.

_____ 4. You two must have something very special.

_____ 5. Time goes by slowly when you're not here.

_____ 6. Writing doesn't seem to be one of your favorite pastimes, but I hope to hear from you soon.

Event

A. Wedding
B. Death
C. Birthday
D. Wedding anniversary
E. Golden wedding anniversary
F. Friendship
G. Love
H. Illness

_____ 7. Here's to another 50 years
together.

_____ 8. May you soon be out of bed
and back on the tennis court.

Now You Do It   Complete this practice dialogue. You wish to buy a card for your mother's birthday. Ask the salesperson to help you.

YOU: _____ ?

SALESPERSON: Yes. The birthday cards are right over here.

YOU: _____ .

SALESPERSON: Are you looking for a particular kind of card? We have sentimental cards, humorous cards, and even cards that are written especially for mothers.

YOU: _____ .

SALESPERSON: That is an excellent choice. I hope she likes it.

YOU: _____ .

4   Going Out With Friends

In North America, there are many kinds of social events to take part in. Some events are casual and others are formal. However, they all offer challenges to guests regarding what they should do and how they should respond to invitations.

Matching: Social Events   Here are some terms used to describe social events or phrases that are used on invitations. (Some hints for proper dress are included.) Match them with the correct definition. The answers are on page 180.

_____ 1. B.Y.O.B.

_____ 2. R.S.V.P.

_____ 3. Regrets only

_____ 4. Cocktail party

_____ 5. Prom

_____ 6. Wedding reception

A. A party at which guests play card games like bridge, euchre, poker, or gin (casual dress)

B. A party held at someone's home in the early afternoon or evening and at which light refreshments are served (suit, nice dress)

C. Respond to the invitation only if you are *not* coming

D. A party for an honored guest who is not told before the party (dress varies)

E. Please let the host know whether or not you will attend

F. A party for an expectant mother to which everyone brings a gift (women only—casual dress)

_____ 7. Wedding ceremony

_____ 8. Baby shower

_____ 9. Potluck dinner

_____ 10. Mixer

_____ 11. Open house

_____ 12. Surprise party

_____ 13. Card party

_____ 14. Graduation party

_____ 15. Picnic

_____ 16. Cookout

G. A party to introduce men and women (dress varies)

H. Bring your own bottle (if you wish to drink wine or liquor)

I. A dinner to which everyone brings a prepared food to share (casual dress)

J. A formal dance for a high school graduation (formal dress—tuxedo, evening gown)

K. The ceremony at which two people are married (suit, nice dress)

L. The party after a wedding (suit, nice dress)

M. A party at which light refreshments and alcoholic beverages are served (suit, nice dress)

N. A party to honor someone who has recently graduated from high school or college (dress varies, but usually casual)

O. An informal gathering at which meat is cooked over an open fire or outdoor grill and served with salads and potato chips (casual dress)

P. A packed lunch, usually consisting of sandwiches, fried chicken, potato or bean salad, and dessert; eaten in a park or open field (very informal dress)

Let's Share   What are some important social events in your country? How are they different from those in North America? In the chart below, give two examples and provide information telling a visitor to your country how to act, what to bring, and what to wear to the social event. When you have finished, share the information with your class. Be prepared to answer questions and to give examples.

Event	What Happens	What to Bring	What to Wear	When to Arrive
1.				

Box continued on the following page

Event	What Happens	What to Bring	What to Wear	When to Arrive
2.				

Quick Customs Quiz

Below are situations in which you might find yourself in North America. Read each situation, decide what is appropriate, and choose the answer that best fits the circumstance. Draw a circle around the letter in front of your answer. Check your answers against those on page 181, which are the answers an American or a Canadian would probably give. (If there is more than one correct answer, circle all that apply.)

1. You are over 21 and invited to a friend's house for dinner. What should you take?

   a. A bottle of wine.
   b. Flowers for the host.
   c. Nothing.
   d. Some food to cook.
   e. A friend or a relative.
   f. Your children.
   g. A gift costing more than $10.

2. You are eating dinner at a friend's house or in a restaurant. Where should you keep your hands when you are not holding eating utensils?

   a. In your lap.
   b. On the table.
   c. By your side.

3. You are an adult who has been invited to an open house. What do you expect it to be like?

   a. The men talking in one room and the women in another.
   b. Men and women talking together.
   c. Everyone standing.
   d. Everyone sitting.
   e. Men and women drinking liquor.
   f. A quiet atmosphere.
   g. A noisy atmosphere.

4. When you are eating with others around a table, which of the following should you do?

   a. Carry on a conversation.
   b. Eat in silence.
   c. Make smacking noises and other eating noises to show that you are enjoying the meal.
   d. Burp to show that you enjoyed the meal.
   e. Chew with your mouth closed.
   f. Talk with food in your mouth.

5. You are invited to a friend's home for dinner. After you eat the food you are served, you are still hungry and would like more. What should you do?

   a. Wait for the friend to ask you several times if you want "seconds" (a second helping of food).

   b. Accept the friend's first offer of seconds and say, "Yes, thank you. It's delicious."

   c. Help yourself to more food.

   d. Don't eat any more because the host will think you are impolite or unable to get enough to eat at home.

6. A friend says to you, "Let's go out to dinner sometime." What does he or she mean?

   a. He or she will pay for both dinners.

   b. You will pay for both dinners.

   c. Each of you will pay for your own dinner.

7. When a friend says, "Why don't you come over and visit sometime," what does he or she mean?

   a. You may go to this friend's house whenever you want.

   b. Your friend is making pleasant conversation but is not inviting you to visit.

8. You wish to attract the waiter's attention in a restaurant. What should you do?

   a. Snap your fingers.

   b. Tap your glass with your spoon.

   c. Catch the waiter's eye and raise your hand.

   d. Whistle.

   e. Shout out the waiter's name.

   f. Call out, "Waiter" or "Sir."

9. You and your friend have ordered an alcoholic beverage at a disco, bar, or restaurant. Before he will serve you, the waiter asks to see your identification. What should you show him?

   a. Your driver's license.

   b. Your social security card.

   c. Your passport.

   d. Your school ID card.

   e. Your cash or traveler's checks.

10. The waiter has left your check on the table. How can you pay for it?

   a. Cash.

   b. Personal check.

   c. Credit card.

   d. Money from your country.

   e. Traveler's checks.

11. There appears to be a $2.50 charge on your check for an item that you did not order. What should you do?

   a. Forget it. It's not worth bothering about.

   b. Get the waiter and tell him that there appears to be a mistake on your bill.

   c. Get angry and demand that the waiter correct the mistake immediately.

   d. Ask for the manager or headwaiter (also sometimes called the *maitre d*).

   e. Pay the bill, and when you get home write a letter to the restaurant explaining the problem.

Let's Share

When you checked your answers you may have been surprised at some of the answers to the *Quick Customs Quiz* because they are different from the actions that would be acceptable in your country. Choose two items that would be handled differently at home and explain how and why those actions would be appropriate. Then share your answers with the class.

1. Question _____

_____

_____

_____

_____

_____

2. Question _____

_____

_____

_____

_____

_____

5   The Concept of Time

You are invited to a friend's house for dinner at 6:00 P.M. What time should you arrive?
a. 5:30 P.M. b. 6:00 P.M. c. 7:00 P.M.
These are the reactions you might get if you arrived at these times:

5:30 P.M.   6:00 P.M.   7:00 P.M.

In North America, time is exact. People plan activities and arrange their lives around specific times. For example, you should always arrive exactly on time for dinner, a date, or a business appointment. While it is sometimes acceptable to arrive five minutes early, it is considered extremely impolite to arrive late. If other people are expected for dinner or for a meeting and you are late, everyone else will have to wait until you arrive to begin.

Let's Share
As you can see, in North America you are expected to arrive a little early or on time. However, in many cultures time is more flexible. Write five rules for time in your culture. Be sure to include specific situations and reasons.

1. _____

   _____

2. _____

   _____

3. _____

   _____

4. _____

   _____

5. _____

   _____

When you have finished, share this information with the class.

Now You Do It
Complete these conversations.

1. Jim is inviting you to dinner.

   JIM: I'd like you to have dinner with my family this Saturday night.

   YOU: _____.

   JIM: That's great! Can you be at my house at 6:30 P.M.?

   YOU: _____.

   JIM: I live at 420 Elm Street.

   YOU: _____?

   JIM: Well, you go out Culver Road until you get to Main Street and then turn left. It's the second street on the right.

   YOU: _____?

   JIM: Oh, you don't need to bring anything but yourself!

   YOU: Thanks for inviting me.

JIM: _____

YOU: See you at 6:30 P.M. on Saturday.

JIM: _____

2. Sometimes you're unable to arrive on time even though you try to. Call your host, explain your reasons for being late, and give the time that you will arrive. (In this dialogue, you have gotten lost.)
(*Telephone rings.*)

JIM: Hello.

YOU: _____

JIM: Yes, we were wondering where you were. What happened?

YOU: _____

JIM: Where are you? Maybe I can give you directions to get here from where you are.

YOU: _____

JIM: Gee, you really *are* lost! The best thing to do is to drive back down Culver Road until you get to East High School and then turn left.

YOU: _____

JIM: Yes, that's about two miles. After you turn left at the high school, Elm Street will be the second street on your right. Understand? Repeat the directions back to me to make sure that you've got them.

YOU: _____.

JIM: That's right. If you still can't find it, call me and I'll come get you. It's no trouble.

YOU: Thanks a lot. I'll be there by 7:30, I hope. I'm really sorry to be so much trouble.

JIM: _____.

Role-Play Choose partners and role-play each of these situations. Be certain to use correct body language and facial expressions.

1. You and your friend have decided to attend a party, but neither of you is sure what time you should arrive. Ask the person giving the party about the correct time to come.
2. You plan to attend a very popular movie, and there are very long lines of people waiting to buy tickets. Decide with a friend whether you should attend the 7:30 P.M. or 9:45 P.M. show and what time you should arrive at the theater to get your tickets.
3. You wish to attend church services. Telephone the church office and ask the times of the services.

Formal Restaurant

Some people, instead of inviting you to their home, will suggest going to a restaurant. Eating out is a difficult experience if you are unfamiliar with the foods or the idioms used to order them. Here are some phrases and idioms to help you place an order at a restaurant.

WAITER: Can I bring you something else, sir?

DINER: Yes, thank you. Can we see the dessert menu, please?

Fast Food Restaurant

WAITRESS: What'll it be?

PATRON: I'd like a cheeseburger, an order of fries, and a chocolate shake.

WAITRESS: For here or to go?

PATRON: To go.

As you can see, the language you use differs in each situation. In a less formal environment, you may speak in a more open, friendly manner. In the following exercise, you will get practice responding in both formal and informal situations.

Family Restaurant

WAITRESS: Would you like to see the children's menu? patron

YES, PLEASE.

Now You Do It

Complete each dialogue. Then role-play them with a partner. Be sure to use correct gestures and body language.

1. You go to a coffee shop and order ice cream. The waiter brings you a glass of icedtea instead.

YOU: _____.

WAITER: Yes. What can I do for you?

YOU: _____.

WAITER: No. I'm certain you ordered iced tea.

YOU: _____.

WAITER: I'm sorry. I'll bring you your ice cream. What flavor do you want?

YOU: _____.

WAITER: Can I get you anything else?

YOU: _____.

2. You are in a restaurant and see something on the menu that looks interesting, but you don't know what it is. Ask the waiter to explain the dish to you.

YOU: _____.

WAITER: Yes, sir. How can I help you?

YOU: _____?

WAITER: That is a beef patty cooked to your order and served on a seeded bun with our special sauce.

YOU: _____?

WAITER: Well, the special sauce is made of mayonnaise, catsup, pickles, and several spices.

YOU: _____?

WAITER: I believe you would enjoy it. How would you like it cooked? Rare, medium, or well-done?

YOU: _____?

WAITER: Rare means the inside of the meat is very red, medium means the inside is pink, and well-done means the meat is cooked completely.

YOU: _____.

WAITER: Thank you. I'll bring your order shortly.

3. You are on a date with a friend at a restaurant. Decide what you wish to order from the menu and order it.

DATE: There seem to be a lot of delicious items to choose from. What are you thinking of ordering?

YOU: _____?

DATE: Well, I think I'll have the lasagna. They really make it well here.

YOU: _____?

DATE: Their stuffed shells are good, too. You can get them stuffed with ricotta cheese or with meat.

YOU: _____.

DATE: They both **do** sound good. Maybe if you get the stuffed shells, we could share.

YOU: _____.

DATE: That sounds like a good idea.

YOU: _____.

DATE: When the waitress comes back we'll order our dinner. What should we have to drink?

YOU: _____.

DATE: I'll have that too. This should be a great dinner!

4. You are in the cafeteria or a fast-food restaurant. Order a sandwich of roast beef and lettuce on rye bread, without mayonnaise.

SERVER: What'll you have?

YOU: _____.

SERVER: What kind of bread?

YOU: _____.

SERVER: Do you want anything on it?

YOU: _____.

SERVER: Did you say you want lettuce and tomato?

YOU: _____.

5. You are in a fast-food restaurant (McDonald's or Burger King). You have been waiting in line, and now it's your turn. Order a hamburger with ketchup, no onions, french fries, and a large Cola.

SERVER: Can I help you?

YOU: _____.

SERVER: To eat here or to go?

YOU: _____.

SERVER: Do you want extra catsup or salt? The packages are on that counter over there. Help yourself.

YOU: _____.

SERVER: That'll be $2.45, please.

Role-Play Choose partners and role-play each of these situations.

1. You have been invited to a potluck dinner. Ask your host what you should bring, when the dinner starts, and what to wear.
2. A friend has offered to "fix you up with a blind date" for Saturday night. Ask your friend about this person and get him or her to suggest a place to go with your blind date when you go out.

Leave-Taking

The proper way to leave a party or social gathering is to say good-bye to the hosts and to thank them. Here are some examples of leave-taking.

Model dialogues

1. GUEST: Thank you for a lovely evening.

   HOST: I'm so glad you could come.

   GUEST: Good-bye.

   HOST: Good-bye.

2. GUEST: Thank you for inviting me. I had a very good time.

   HOST: So did we. Come visit us again soon.

   GUEST: I'd like that. Thanks again. Good-bye.

   HOST: Good-bye.

3. GUEST: I have to go now. Thank you for the delicious meal.

   HOST: You're very welcome. I'm glad you enjoyed it.

   GUEST: 'Bye

   HOST: Good-bye.

Now You Do It

After you have studied the examples of leave-taking, complete these dialogues. Then practice them with a partner, using correct gestures and body language. Remember to smile and shake hands as you leave.

1. You have attended a dinner party at your professor's house and are ready to leave.

   YOU: _____.

   HOST: I'm so glad you enjoyed the dinner and meeting some new friends.

   YOU: _____.

   HOST: Thank you. I hope you'll come visit us again soon.

   YOU: _____.

   HOST: Good-bye.

2. You have an appointment at 10:00 A.M. It is now 9:30, and you are sitting and talking with friends. Tell them that you have to leave.

   YOU: _____.

   FRIEND: Why? It's only 9:30.

   YOU: _____.

   FRIEND: Too bad. We're having such a good time.

   YOU: _____.

   FRIEND: So long. See you in class.

   YOU: _____.

**What's Going
On Here?** Read the following three-part story about Joe and Al, college roommates in the United
States. After each part, answer the *Discussion Questions* with your classmates. Read these
situations and discuss what went wrong and why.

Part 1

Joe, an international student attending school in the United States had an American
roommate named Al. The two had become very good friends. As Thanksgiving approached, Joe could hear Al talking with his family about how he was looking forward
to going home for the holidays.

Al always got off the phone in an excited mood. He'd say, "Boy, I can't wait to go
home! My Mom makes the best turkey and my grandmother's sweet-potato pie is great."

Whenever Al began to talk like that, Joe would become very quiet, and soon he'd
say, "I'm going to the library" or "I have to do my laundry."

Soon the two, who had been such good friends, weren't spending much time
together and they hardly spoke anymore. In fact, one day Al overheard Joe saying, "Al
has changed. He's really not so nice. I don't like to be around him anymore."

Al was very surprised to hear that, and he asked Joe why he had been acting so
strangely. Joe, of course, said he wasn't acting strangely at all. He said it was **Al** who was
acting strangely.

Discussion questions

1. What was the problem?
2. Who was acting strangely?
3. Why were the two not getting along anymore?
4. Who was at fault?
5. Why?
6. What could either of them have done to improve the situation?

Part 2

One day Al asked Joe what he was going to do over the Thanksgiving holidays since there
would be a four-day weekend.

Joe said he had no plans; he'd stay at school and catch up on some work. Al said,
"Gee it's going to be dead around here. Everyone is going home. There'll be no one left
on this floor."

Joe, starting to get up, said, "Listen, I have work to do. I'm going to the library."

Suddenly, Al said, "Hey, why don't you come home with me? My Mom loves to
have company, and she always makes a big turkey. It would be great to have you meet
my family. After all, I talk about them all the time so you practically know them. And I
know they are dying to meet you."

Joe smiled and said, "Really? Do you mean it? I'd like that, but you'd better ask your
mother first." He smiled, sat down on the bed, and began to watch television with Al

Discussion questions

1. What caused the change in the relationship between Joe and Al?
2. Why was Joe getting ready to go to the library?

3. What made him change his mind?
4. Have you ever been in a similar situation?

Part 3

At Al's house on Thanksgiving Day, Joe met Al's parents and grandparents. He also met Al's two sisters and his three aunts, three uncles, and eight cousins. They sat in the living room talking and laughing and eating hors d'oeuvres of cheese and crackers, fresh vegetables and dip, and some other things which weren't familiar to Joe. They watched football and talked.

At three o'clock, Al's mother said the turkey was ready and everyone should come into the dining room. The table was set with a lot of chairs. There was another table in the kitchen where six of the younger children sat. On the table at each place there were several plates and a lot of silverware. Joe wasn't sure which utensils to use first, so he watched everyone else.

It was a wonderful meal. They had fresh fruit, turkey, mashed potatoes with gravy, cranberry sauce, sweet-potato pie, string beans, and applie pie. Joe took only a little bit at first. He wasn't sure he'd like it. But he did. When Al's mother asked if he wanted more, he said, "No, thank you" very politely. She said, "Al, I'm afraid your friend doesn't like it."

Joe's face turned red. "Oh no," he protested. "I like it very much."

Al's mother never asked him again if he'd like more, and while others kept saying, "Pass me the potatoes" or "Can I have the cranberry sauce?" he sat quietly watching and wishing he could have more of the delicious dinner.

1. What was the problem?
2. Did he really like the food?
3. If he did, why didn't he take more?
4. If he didn't, why did he say he did?

Exploring North America

A. Choose a North American holiday that interests you. Either by asking your North American friends or by doing research, discover different things that families do to celebrate the holiday.

B. Rather than writing letters, people in North America send greeting cards for many occasions—everything from wishing friends a merry Christmas to "friendship cards" encouraging closeness in relationships. Go to a North American store that sells greeting cards, and examine several cards for a particular occasion; for example, you might look at birthday cards. Note the types of cards (serious, informal, funny, insulting) that are available. Describe one card you would choose to send and one you wouldn't. Give your reasons in both cases. What do the variety and types of cards tell you about North American culture and attitudes?

C. One of the most popular pastimes in North America is eating out. One survey found that Americans eat one meal in five in a restaurant. Consult your local telephone book and ask your North American friends to help you make a list of good places to eat in your town. Find out about places for both formal and informal dining. Ask your friends why they like a particular restaurant and what dishes they would recommend.

Speaking Out

A. One of the greatest expenses a family has to meet is the cost of their daughter's wedding. In Canada and the United States, most of the wedding expenses are paid by the bride's family. These days, the cost of a formal wedding is around $10,000. The wedding dress, which is only worn once, usually costs more than $1,000. The "wedding industry" is so important that several magazines are published which deal only with weddings, and thousands of stores sell only bridal attire.

Many families must borrow money to pay for weddings. As one father-of-the-bride said, "This three-hour wedding and reception will take ten years for us to pay for." Paying back the money may cause great hardships on the parents or the couple who pays for their wedding.

1. Do you think that the cost of an expensive wedding is justified? Why or why not?
2. Who do you think should pay for the wedding? Why?
3. Ask your North American friends how they feel about formal weddings and what kind of ceremony they had or would like to have. Ask them their reasons. Discuss your findings with the class.
4. What do these attitudes toward formal weddings tell you about the culture? Why?

B. The United States has more "special" days and holidays than any other country. Some of the special days which require a card or gift are Secretary's Day and Boss's Day. Other special days include National Ice Cream Day, Teacher's Day, Grandparent's Day, and even Groundhog Day.

Some people feel that the special days, which require gift-giving, are created by businesses and advertising agencies to force the consumer to buy products, such as cards, flowers, and gifts, rather than to honor a person or an occasion.

1. How do you feel about these special, gift-giving days? Why?
2. If you had the chance to select five North American holidays or special days to celebrate, which would you choose? Why?
3. Ask your North American friends how they feel about these special, gift-giving days. Discuss their answers with the class.

C. Looking at a display of Christmas merchandise arranged in a large department store in August, a shopper exclaimed, "My goodness, Christmas is certainly coming early this year!"

It is not unusual for merchants in some countries to begin displaying Christmas merchandise in September, Thanksgiving items in August, and Easter articles in January. Some people say that this early display of seasonal items "rushes the season" and causes them to tire of the holiday before it comes. Merchants, however, say that having merchandise available early allows people to make better gift choices and stimulates them to buy more products, which helps the economy.

1. Go to local department stores and determine which holiday merchandise is being displayed. Ask the clerk when they first began to display seasonal items. Compare your findings with those of other class members.
2. Ask a North American friend how he or she feels about early display ("rushing the season") of holiday items and the effect it has on that person as a consumer. Discuss your answers with the class.
3. What do you think about early displays of seasonal merchandise? Why?
4. People in North America like to plan for every event. Now, they can even plan, and prepay for, their own funerals. Many funeral homes offer a service called a "pre-need program," in which customers can select their casket, clothing, funeral service, type of embalming, cemetery plot, and headstone. Customers can make a choice so that their family will not have to make arrangements when they die. The cost of a funeral can vary from about $1,200 to over $10,000.

   a. Why do you think people would want to buy such a program? What are some of the purposes that it can serve for people and their families?
   b. What do you think about the "pre-need programs"? Would you be interested in having one? Why?
   c. Who do you think devised "pre-need programs"? For what reason? Who benefits from the plan?
   d. What do these "prepay programs" tell you about North American customs, attitudes, and culture?

Seven

Shopping

Which of these items would you expect to find in a large North American grocery store?

Fresh vegetables
Meats
Magazines
Baked goods
Clothing
Fabric
Soap and waxes
Dog and cat food
Diapers
Batteries
Imported foods
Snack foods
Cereals

Flowers and gardening supplies
Cards and wrapping paper
Paper products
Medicines
Toys
Dishes and silverware
Small appliances
Rat poison and bug killers
Small tools
Books
Frozen foods
Salad bars
Potted plants

You would probably find all of them!

1 | Places to Shop

Shopping in North America is exciting and challenging. The consumer is offered an almost limitless selection of merchandise in all price ranges and sizes. Through shopping, you can sharpen your English skills as you ask questions, select products, and sometimes even bargain for the best price at garage sales and farm markets.

Exploring North America Visit several stores, examine newspaper and television advertisements, and ask other students the best places to buy the following items. List at least two stores where you can buy each group of items.

Items	Stores
1. Trees, plants, gardening supplies, fertilizer	
2. Parts for fixing cars and trucks	
3. Strings for a guitar	
4. Rings, precious stones, necklaces	
5. Bread, rolls, cakes, cookies	
6. Vacation and travel information	
7. Tools, supplies for maintaining the home	
8. Tables, chairs, lamps, carpets, beds	
9. Information on loans, checking accounts, and the exchange rate	

Other Shopping Options

Besides regular retail stores, there are other places to shop where items are often less expensive.

Lawn sale ⎫ Garage sale ⎪ Porch sale ⎬ Yard sale ⎪ Household sale ⎭	People sell used merchandise at their home. They set up the sale in the yard, garage, or driveway, or on the porch.
Farmer's market	Farmers bring their farm produce to one location to sell. Foods are usually fresher and less expensive than in a store.
Flea market	People sell antiques, used merchandise, and new items at discounted prices.

These sales are often listed in the "want-ads" section of the newspaper. At such sales, you may bargain for a lower price.

Shopping from Catalogs

Shopping from catalogs has become an important way of buying all kinds of items, from exotic foods to large appliances. Some of the best-known catalogs are from Montgomery Ward, L.L. Bean, and Swiss Colony. Can you think of any other catalogs? What do the companies sell? Write your answers here.

_____

_____

To order from a catalog, follow these instructions.

1. If you are not familiar with the catalog company, ask your friends what they have heard about the quality of the products and the company's customer-service policies **before** you place an order. It is better to learn negative things about a company before you buy a product than afterwards.
2. Look through the catalog and note any items you want to order.
3. Turn to the section of the catalog that tells you how to order. Read the instructions for filling out the order blank, including how to add sales tax and shipping and handling charges and how to pay for your purchase. Some catalogs also list a number you can call to place your order by phone.
4. Fill out the form carefully. Check to make sure you put in the correct number, size, amount, and description of each product you are buying. Add all required shipping fees and sales tax.
5. Enclose a check or money order for the correct amount. **Never send cash in the mail!** If you are ordering by phone, you must have a credit card to pay for your purchase. Have your card ready so that you can give them the information they ask for from your credit card.
6. Keep a copy of your order, so you'll have a record in case a problem arises.
7. Carefully read the section of the catalog that tells you what to do if you are not satisfied with your order.

Ordering Merchandise from Television or Radio Advertisements

Often, when you are watching television or listening to the radio, you will hear advertisements inviting you to order merchandise. If you want to order something, carefully write down the address of the company and an exact description of the product and its cost.

To order by mail, send a check or money order made out to the company, along with a description of the product and your name and address. Include your zip code. **Do not send cash** in the mail. Keep a copy of your order and method of payment in case you do not receive the product or are not satisfied with it.

If you wish to order by phone, you must have a credit card. Most companies take MasterCard, Visa, or Discover Card. When you call, have your credit card ready so you can give the required information from your credit card. Keep a record of your order.

Ordering Merchandise over the phone

Here is a conversation model in which someone orders merchandise over the phone. Practice the model with a classmate.

SALESPERSON: Hello. This is Country Products of Missouri. How can I help you?

YOU: I would like to order item number 4896B, which appeared in your Christmas catalog on page 36.

SALESPERSON: That would be the women's snowflake print wool sweater.

YOU: Yes. I would like to order it in size 12 and in royal blue.

SALESPERSON: That's a lovely sweater. We have it in stock, and it should reach you in about ten days. Is there anything else you want to order?

YOU: No, thank you.

SALESPERSON: Which credit card do you wish to use to pay for your purchase?

YOU: I want to use my Chase Visa card.

SALESPERSON: Please give me your name as it appears on the credit card.

YOU: Ann T. Dowell.

SALESPERSON: Please spell your last name for me.

YOU: D-O-W-E-L-L.

SALESPERSON: Thank you. Please tell me the number of your card and the date it expires.

YOU: 4356-67-9087 is the number. The card expires on August 8, 1996.

SALESPERSON: Thank you. Please tell me your address and the address you wish the sweater sent to.

YOU: Please send the sweater to me at 436 North Plain Street, Brownsville, Missouri 65790.

SALESPERSON: Thank you for ordering from Country Products of Missouri. Your order will reach you in about ten days. If you are not satisfied with the sweater for any reason, please return it to us with your receipt and we will replace it or credit your account.

YOU: Thank you. I'm looking forward to receiving the sweater. Good-bye.

SALESPERSON: Good-bye.

Exploring North America

Bring to class a mail-order catalog from a North American company. Share your catalog with other members of the class. Read the catalogs carefully and compare the following information. Afterward, practice ordering items from the catalogs.

1. The types of merchandise offered in the catalogs
2. The quality of the merchandise offered in the catalogs
3. The prices of similar items in the catalogs, to determine which catalog offers the best values
4. The guarantees that companies offer on their products
5. The added charges, such as shipping and handling, that companies add to the cost of their items

2 Making Your Purchase

Once you have selected the item you want to purchase, you may pay for it in several ways. You may even be able to save money on your purchase by using a store or manufacturer's coupon.

Ways to Pay	*What You Should Know*
1. U.S. or Canadian Currency	Few businesses, except those near the U.S.-Canadian border, accept currencies of other nations.
2. Personal checks	These checks are issued by your bank, and they allow you to draw from the money you have on deposit. You should be prepared to show identification when you pay by personal check. Some businesses will only take checks drawn on local banks.
3. Traveler's checks	Most businesses will accept traveler's checks issued by banks. Be prepared to show identification, such as your passport, to establish your identity. Never sign your traveler's check until you are ready to pay for your purchase. Keep a record of the checks you use.
4. Credit cards	The most common national credit cards are Visa, MasterCard, and Discover Card. These are issued through banks to individuals with good credit. Many businesses, like Sears and J.C. Penney, have their own credit cards which they issue to their customers. These cards can only be used in the store which issues the credit card. Interest rates vary from 10 percent to 27 percent per year on the unpaid balance for the purchased items.
5. Layaway	This is a way to buy an item when you do not have the money to pay for it immediately. You choose an item and make a "down payment," which is usually at least 10 percent of the item's value. Then you make payments each month until you have paid for the item and can take it home from the store.

Shopping with Coupons

You can save money by shopping with coupons. You can find coupons like the ones below in newspapers, on circulars which come in the mail, on packages, or in the telephone book.

If you read the coupon, you will find that most contain the following information:

1. What product or service you can purchase with the coupon
2. How much you save when you use the coupon
3. When you can use the coupon
4. Where you can use the coupon
5. Who can use the coupon
6. Restrictions on the use of the coupon

Here is an example of a store coupon.

Here is an example of a manufacturer's coupon.

Examine the coupon below, and then answer the questions which follow.

1. Where can you use the coupon?
2. How much will you save when you use the coupon?
3. When can you use the coupon?
4. What do you get when you use the coupon?
5. What are the restrictions on the use of the coupon?
6. Who can use the coupon?

Putting an Item on Layaway

Here is a model conversation in which someone put an item on layaway. Practice the model with a classmate.

YOU: I would like to put this jacket on layaway.

SALESPERSON: Total amount due on this purchase is $120. If you put $20 down now, you can make five payments of $20 per payment and the jacket will be yours.

YOU: That sounds fine. Do you charge interest?

SALESPERSON: No. All we ask is that you make your payments on time. If you don't make your payements, you will lose whatever you have paid on the jacket.

YOU: Thank you. I didn't know that.

SALESPERSON: Do you want to make your payments weekly or monthly?

YOU: I'll make my payments each week.

Making a Purchase at a Department Store

Here is a conversation model in which someone talks with a salesperson. Practice these models with a classmate.

1. YOU: Excuse me, can you tell me where the dresses are?

   SALESPERSON: Do you want children's, juniors', or misses' dresses?

   YOU: I don't know the difference.

   SALESPERSON: Children's has clothes for infants and children through age 10 or 11. Juniors' are for teens and women who are small. Misses are for regular-size women.

   YOU: I see. Where are the juniors' dresses located?

2. SALESPERSON: Can I help you?

   YOU: No, thank you. I'm just looking.

3. SALESPERSON: Can I help you?

   YOU: Yes, I'd like to pay for this. Can you tell me how much the sales tax on this item is?

   SALESPERSON: The sales tax is 7 percent.

   YOU: Thank you.

   SALESPERSON: Did you know that for sanitary reasons you can't return bathing suits or underwear?

   YOU: Thanks for telling me. May I have a box instead of a bag for the bathing suit?

   SALESPERSON: Certainly. Is this purchase cash, check, or credit card?

   YOU: Cash.

3 Talking with Salespeople

Quick Customs Quiz

Below are situations in which you might find yourself in the United States or Canada. Read each situation, decide what is appropriate, and choose the answer that best fits the circumstance. Draw a circle around the letter in front of your answer. Check your answers against those on page 181, which are the answers an American or a Canadian would probably give. If there is more than one correct answer, circle all that apply.

1. You are in a department store because you wish to look but have no intention of buying anything. A salesperson comes up to you and asks, "Can I help you?" What should you do?

   a. Say no.
   b. Say yes and ask for help so you won't offend the salesperson.
   c. Say, "Thanks, but I'm just browsing."

2. When reading a newspaper or magazine, you notice something called a manufacturer's coupon; it offers to give you 10 to 15 cents off the price of a grocery-store product. Since you wish to save money, what should you do?

a. Take the whole newspaper to the store and give it to the clerk when you pay for your groceries.

b. When you are paying for your groceries, tell the clerk that you saw the coupon in the paper and want the discount.

c. Neatly cut out the coupon and take it with you to the store. Give it to the clerk when you pay for the product.

3. You see a suit that you really like but think the price is too high. What should you do?

a. If you can afford it for the price, buy it.

b. Offer the clerk less money for it.

c. Tell the clerk that the suit is not worth that much money.

d. Look for the same suit at another store, where it may cost less.

4. You wish to purchase some new clothes in the United States but are not sure of what size you wear in American sizes. What should you do?

a. Ask the salesperson for help.

b. Try on clothes until you find the size that fits you.

c. Ask friends who have been living in North America longer what size you should wear.

5. You find a garment that you really like but are not sure that it will fit you. What should you do?

a. Buy it. You can always return if it doesn't fit.

b. Put it on over your clothes.

c. Measure it against your body.

d. Take it to the rest room and try it on.

e. Ask to try it on in a fitting room.

6. You wish to buy a used car and have just found the one you want on a used-car lot. The salesman offers you a 30-day warranty and will reduce the price by $100. What should you do?

a. Ask a mechanic who does not work at the used car lot to check the car to make sure that it's in good condition.

b. Go to other used-car lots to compare prices on similar cars.

c. Buy the car before someone else does.

d. Ask the salesman to lower the price by another $50 or more.

e. Ask to have the warranty in writing and make sure you understand what it covers.

Idioms and Phrases

Here are some phrases you will find helpful when you need to ask for information. The words in bold face are key phrases that can be adapted both to ask questions and to answer them.

1. YOU: **Can you recommend** a gift I can send my sister?

SALESPERSON: Perhaps she'd like some perfume.

2. YOU: **What** other colors do these shirts come in?

SALESPERSON: They come in red, blue, and white.

3. YOU: **Can you tell me** what size I need to buy?

SALESPERSON: I think a medium would fit you well.

4. YOU: **How do I** return this if it does not match the color of my living room?

   SALESPERSON: Bring your receipt and we'll refund your money or exchange it for one in another color.

5. YOU: **Where can I find** the corn flakes?

   SALESPERSON: They're in aisle 2.

Now You Do It   Complete these practice dialogues. Then role-play them with a partner, using correct gestures and body language.

1. Ask the pharmacist to recommend an effective dandruff shampoo.

   PHARMACIST: Hello. Can I help you?

   YOU: _____.

   PHARMACIST: There are several brands available. What are your symptoms?

   YOU: _____.

   PHARMACIST: I see. Well, you could try Ridruff or Hair and Scalp.

   YOU: _____?

   PHARMACIST: Ridruff is medicated and costs a dollar more than Hair and Scalp. But either shampoo will do the job, I think.

   YOU: _____?

   PHARMACIST: The shampoos are located on the third shelf, beside the hair sprays.

   _____.

2. You want to buy some perfume as a gift for your friend Ann's birthday. Ask a mutual friend, Debbie, what kind of perfume **she** uses, because you like the way her perfume smells.

   YOU: _____?

   DEBBIE: Fine. How's it going?

   YOU: _____.

   DEBBIE: That is a problem. Sometimes I have trouble getting presents for my friends, too.

   YOU: _____?

   DEBBIE: Thanks a lot. It's nice of you to notice. My perfume is called Wintersong.

   YOU: _____?

   DEBBIE: Yes, I think Ann will like it.

   YOU: _____.

   DEBBIE: Okay. See you later.

3. You have an advertisement you cut out of the newspaper, and you wish to have a salesperson help you find the merchandise.

YOU: _____?

SALESPERSON: Yes, they're over here.

YOU: I can't find my size. Do you have any more sweaters?

SALESPERSON: No, we . . .

YOU: I want the sweater you have advertised, not a higher-priced one.

SALESPERSON: Well, I can give you a "rain check."

YOU: _____?

SALESPERSON: Yes, you can buy the sweater at the same price when we get it in stock.

YOU: _____?

SALESPERSON: Probably later in the week.

YOU: _____.

4 Problems and Solutions

Sometimes, even though you have shopped carefully, you must return an item to the store or have it repaired by the store. Here are some informative situations that will help you deal with these problems.

Quick Customs Quiz   Below are situations in which you might find yourself in the United States or Canada. Read each situation, decide what is appropriate, and choose the answer that best fits the circumstance. Draw a circle around the letter in front of your answer. Check your answers against those on page 182, which are the answers an American or a Canadian would probably give.

1. You wish to return something you bought a month ago. You've never used it but haven't had the opportunity to bring it back. At the store, the clerk tells you that since you bought the item more than seven days ago, you cannot return it. What should you do?

   a. Show the clerk that the tickets are still on the item and that you haven't used it.
   b. Ask to see the manager.
   c. Tell the clerk you'll never shop in the store again.
   d. Explain that you didn't know that merchandise had to be returned within seven days.
   e. Thank the clerk and leave.

2. You received a shirt as a gift for your birthday. You like the shirt but find it is too small. What should you do?

   a. Keep it because it is a gift.
   b. Go to the store where your friend bought the shirt and exchange it for a larger size.
   c. Tell your friend to get you a larger size.
   d. Give it to someone else as a gift.

3. You've bought a refrigerator and it breaks down during the first 30 days you own it. A friend tells you not to worry because the refrigerator is under warranty. What does this mean, and what should you do?

   a. The store where you bought it will fix the refrigerator for free, so you should call and tell them about it.
   b. If the refrigerator is broken through normal use, you should call the manufacturer, tell them the appliance is under warranty, and ask them to fix it.
   c. You should call a service company and have the machine fixed.

4. You have been receiving magazines in the mail that you did not order. What should you do?

   a. Write to the company and tell them there has been a mistake.
   b. Send the magazines back.
   c. Keep the magazines and do nothing.
   d. Pay for the magazines when the bill comes.

5. You open a jar of applesauce and inside it you find a few pieces of broken glass. Fortunately, you have not eaten any of the applesauce. What should you do?

   a. Throw it away.
   b. Take out the glass and eat the rest.
   c. Return the applesauce and the jar to the store where you bought it and tell them about the broken glass.

Now You Do It   Complete these conversations. Then practice them aloud with a partner. Be sure to use appropriate gestures and body language. Speak with expression!

1. You wish to return a coat that you purchased by check from a department store.

   YOU: I'd like to return this coat, please.

   SALESPERSON: What's wrong with it?

   YOU: _____.

   SALESPERSON: Okay, do you have your receipt?

   YOU: _____.

   SALESPERSON: Do you want to exchange it for another coat, or do you want your money back?

   YOU: _____.

   SALESPERSON: I'm really sorry you had problems with the coat.

   YOU: _____.

2. You have purchased an expensive watch; after 30 days, it stops working. You have your receipt and want the store to repair or replace it.

SALESPERSON: Can I help you?

YOU: _____.

SALESPERSON: Do you have your receipt?

YOU: _____.

SALESPERSON: Okay, but we can't fix it here. We'll have to send it to Chicago to be repaired.

YOU: _____?

SALESPERSON: It could take as long as three or four months. Is that okay? Service is really slow with this watch manufacturer.

YOU: _____.

SALESPERSON: Well, I'm not sure we can replace it after 30 days. I'll have to ask the manager.

YOU: _____.

SALESPERSON: He says we can replace it but we don't have this watch in stock now. What do you want me to do?

YOU: _____?

SALESPERSON: Yes, we can order you one from our Northside store. That will only take one day. I'm really sorry for all the trouble and wish I could help you today.

YOU: _____.

3. You want to buy a sweater in a department store.

SALESPERSON: Can I help you?

YOU: _____.

SALESPERSON: They're over here. What size do you need?

YOU: _____.

SALESPERSON: Are you looking for a particular color to match something?

YOU: Yes. _____.

SALESPERSON: This one looks like what you've described.

YOU: No, I'd rather have _____.

SALESPERSON: How about this one? Would you like to try it on?

YOU: _____.

SALESPERSON: The fitting rooms are located in the back of this department. I'll take you.

YOU: _____.

SALESPERSON: Let me know if I can help you.

YOU: _____.

4. You want to order merchandise over the telephone. (The person playing **you** should have a Visa, MasterCard, or Discovery Card ready.)

SALESPERSON: Hello, thank you for calling Fashions Unlimited. This is Mark speaking. How can I help you?

YOU: _____.

SALESPERSON: What color and size would you like?

YOU: _____.

SALESPERSON: What else would you like to order?

YOU: _____.

SALESPERSON: Your total for this purchase is $69.80, plus $3.75 shipping and handling. What credit card do you wish to use for this purchase?

YOU: _____.

SALESPERSON: Thank you. Please tell me your credit card number and the expiration date.

YOU: _____.

SALESPERSON: Thank you. Please tell me your name exactly as it appears on the card and the address you want the order shipped to.

YOU: _____.

SALESPERSON: Please spell your name for me.

YOU: _____.

SALESPERSON: Thank you. Your order will reach you in about ten days. Thank you for ordering from Fashions Unlimited.

Role-Play Now that you've practiced shopping using the dialogues, you are ready for the next step, role-playing. Choose a partner and role-play each of the situations below. Discuss the situation first; then decide on appropriate dialogue and practice it, using correct body language and gestures. Then take turns with other class members, and act out the situations.

1. You want to buy your friend a birthday present but do not know his or her size. Ask a salesperson to help you select a shirt for your friend. Be sure to describe your friend carefully, and tell the salesperson the type and color of shirt you are looking for.
2. You are in a hardware store and pay cash for a tool. When you count your change, you find that your change is 87 cents less than it should be. Get the salesclerk to give you the correct change.
3. You get your purchase home from the store and discover that it is damaged. Take it back to the store to get your money back. Be sure to have your receipt with you!

Read each situation and decide what went wrong and why.

What's Going On Here?

Read about Jim's experience buying a car in the United States. Then discuss the questions that follow.

Jim lived in an area in the United States that didn't have public transportation, so he had to buy a car. He went to a number of automobile showrooms and finally found a car he really liked. The salesman said he could have the very car he was admiring.

The salesman asked Jim if he'd like to take the car for a drive, and of course Jim said he'd love to. The salesman gave him the keys to the car, and Jim got in. He was surprised that the salesman let him take the car all by himself!

Jim drove around the block several times and knew that this was the car he wanted to buy. It was expensive; the sign on the car said that with all the options (air conditioning, cruise control, interior lights, and so forth) the car cost $19,500. Jim knew that he could get a car for less money if he ordered one without all the fancy options, but he really liked this car, and if he bought it "on time," paying a little each month, he could afford it.

When he got back to the showroom, Jim told the salesman that he would take the car. The salesman said, "You will? Okay. Do you know how much the car is?"

Jim replied, "Yes, I saw the price on the window and that will be okay, but I want to buy the car on time. Can I do that? What's the interest rate?"

The salesman said, "Sure you can buy the car on time. The current rate is 9 percent." Jim signed the papers, and the car was his.

The next time he went into the showroom, to pick up the car, he noticed that the salespeople stopped what they were doing and looked at him. He could hear them laughing, and he had the feeling that they were laughing at him. A salesman asked if he had any friends who would like to buy a car.

Discussion questions

1. How much money did Jim pay for the car?
2. Why did he buy a car with options he hadn't planned to buy? Did the salesman know Jim didn't want the options?
3. How much interest did Jim pay? Look in the local paper and find out what the current rate of interest is for buying a new car.
4. Why was Jim surprised when the salesman gave him the keys to the car to take it for a test drive? Where was the salesman when Jim took the car out for the drive?
5. What did Jim do that seemed very odd to the salespeople? Why did they stop what they were doing to look at him when he went into the showroom to pick up his car?

Speaking Out

Be prepared to discuss the issues presented.

A. Shoppers are constantly encouraged to used credit cards. You can't buy an airline ticket or rent a car over the phone, for example, without a credit card. Some gasoline stations will only accept credit cards. Often, companies will offer incentives to get people to order and use their credit cards.

After the company that issues the credit card checks the applicant's credit, the company gives the card user a "line of credit." This allows the card user to charge from two hundred dollars' worth of goods and services to many thousands of dollars' worth. Often, credit-card users have many credit cards. This allows them to charge thousands of dollars' worth of goods and services.

While using a credit card allows buyers to get the items they want immediately without paying in full, the credit-card user must pay a high interest rate. This rate is often as high as 29 percent of the unpaid balance owed to the credit-card company. This interest rate is much higher than the interest rate charged by banks. Many credit-card users get in trouble financially by charging more items than they can afford to pay for.

1. Do you think that credit-card companies should be allowed to charge interest that is higher than the bank charges? Why or why not?
2. Should people be allowed to have as many credit cards as they want? Why or why not?
3. What should be done to keep people from charging more items on their credit cards than they can afford to pay for?
4. People who think that they cannot live as well as they would like to on their salary use their credit cards to pay for groceries, tobacco, liquor, and day-to-day necessities. What items should people be allowed to charge? What do you think about using credit cards to buy things which are beyond your means?

B. Wearing "name brands," such as Guess, Calvin Klein, and Nike, has become an important criterion for acceptance by peers. Many teenagers insist that nearly every item they wear have the name of a famous clothing designer or product prominently displayed. If a person wears "no name" brands, he or she is not "in," or accepted. Some people say that this is a symptom of a society that is interested in surface, not substance.

Name brands cost several times more than store brands. For example, a pair of Guess jeans may cost $60, while a pair of department-store jeans of the same quality cost only $25. A pair of Nike tennis shoes may cost $50 more than a lesser-known brand.

As a result of advertising, even small children demand that their parents buy them brand-name clothes rather than store brands. Meeting the acceptance criteria created by advertising and peer pressure often cause financial problems and disagreements in families.

1. Why do you think people buy brand-name clothing?
2. Should parents buy their children brand-name clothing if they cannot comfortably afford to? Why or why not?
3. Do you think that students in your school place too much emphasis on the brands of clothing they wear? How do you know? What brands are most popular?
4. Read this statement: "Young people are more interested in what they wear and how they look than in what they learn and what kind of people they are." From what you have observed, do you agree or disagree with the statement? Give specific examples to support your opinion.

Eight

Using the Telephone

A North American visiting another English-speaking country was expecting few differences when using the telephone. From the airport, she called her friend to pick her up. Although she carefully inserted the correct coins, all she could hear was the person at the other end of the line saying, "Hello, hello, hello!" She tried to explain where she was and what she wanted, but the other person couldn't hear her. Finally, her friend realized what was happening and told her, "If you want to talk, you have to push the button on the phone!"

Have you ever had an experience like this with a telephone? If so, share it with your class.

In this chapter, we'll discuss how to use the telephone for business and social occasions in North America.

1 Learning About the Telephone

Matching: Telephone Terms

There are many terms you will need to know to use the telephone in the United States or Canada. Match the terms in the left-hand column with their meaning in the right-hand column. Check your answers on page 183.

_____ 1. Person-to-person call

_____ 2. Wrong number

_____ 3. Toll-free number

A. Broken; not working
B. The three-digit number preceding a telephone number that indicates the city and area in which it is located
C. A call charged to the person who receives the long-distance call

	4. Area code	D. A long-distance call that the caller dials without help from the operator
	5. Operator	E. A number that is not the number you wished to reach
	6. Unlisted number	F. A telephone number that is neither listed in the telephone book nor available from the operator
	7. Receiver	G. An employee of the telephone company who assists people in making calls
	8. Party line	H. A telephone call made within your calling area, for which there is no charge
	9. Long-distance call	I. The part of the telephone that you hold against your ear to speak and listen
	10. Local call	J. A call made outside your calling area and usually costing more and requiring you to dial 0 or 1 plus the number of the person you're calling
	11. Out of order	K. A telephone connection that is shared by two or more customers and costs less than a private line, which is used by only one customer
	12. Busy signal	L. A long-distance call that is free of charge to the caller (many large businesses and hotels provide such a number, which usually begins with 1-800)
	13. Station-to-station or direct-dial call	M. A call made with operator assistance to a particular person
	14. Collect call	N. A beeping noise that indicates someone is talking on the phone
	15. Call waiting	O. Enables you to answer a second call while placing your first call on hold
	16. Call forwarding	P. Lets you send your calls to another number

Model Dialogues

Talking with the operator:

1. OPERATOR: Hello. This is the operator. Can I help you?

   JEFF: Yes, I'd like to make a person-to-person collect call to Peter Strong at (617) 872-9012. My name is Jeff Bridges.

   OPERATOR: Just a moment. (*makes call*) I have a collect person-to-person call for Peter Strong from Jeff Bridges. Will you accept the charges?

   PETER: Yes, this is Peter Strong. I'll accept the charges.

   OPERATOR: Go ahead, please.

2. OPERATOR: This is the operator. What city, please?

YOU: Boca Raton, Florida.

OPERATOR: Yes, go ahead, please.

YOU: I'd like the phone number of George Snell at 369 Glade Road.

OPERATOR: I'm sorry, that number is unlisted.

YOU: Thank you.

Talking with the Operator

Practice these dialogues with your classmates.

1. Call Directory Assistance ("information"), 411, for the telephone number of Brette Simms, at 1764 Walton Avenue, The Bronx, New York City.

OPERATOR: Operator

YOU: _____.

OPERATOR: You've reached the local operator. Please dial 1 plus area code 212 plus 555-1212 to get that information. A Directory Assistance operator will give you the number.

YOU: _____.

DIRECTORY ASSISTANCE OPERATOR: What city?

YOU: _____.

DIRECTORY ASSISTANCE OPERATOR: Okay. Can I help you?

YOU: I'd like the number for Brette Simms, please.

DIRECTORY ASSISTANCE OPERATOR: How do you spell that name?

YOU: B-R-E-T-T-E S-I-M-M-S.

DIRECTORY ASSISTANCE OPERATOR: Is that *b* as in *boy, r* as in *Robert, e* as in *exit, t* as in *Thomas, t* as in *Thomas, e* as in *exit,* and *s* as in *Susan, i* as in *India, m* as in *money, m* as in *money,* and *s* as in *Susan?*

YOU: _____.

DIRECTORY ASSISTANCE OPERATOR: Do you have an address for the party?

YOU: _____.

INFORMATION OPERATOR: That party can be reached at 299-8063.

YOU: _____.

2. You wish to reverse the charges on a long-distance call. That means that the operator will ask the person you are calling if he or she will pay for the call. Dial 0 plus the ten digits of the number you wish to reach.

OPERATOR: Can I help you?

YOU: _____.

OPERATOR: What is your name, please?

YOU: _____.

OPERATOR: One minute, please. (*phone rings*)

PERSON: Hello.

OPERATOR: This is the operator. I have a collect call from _____.
Will you accept the charges?

PERSON: _____.

OPERATOR: Go ahead.

3. You are away from home and wish to charge a long-distance call to your home phone. Dial 0 plus the ten digits of the number you wish to reach.

OPERATOR: This is the operator. Can I help you?

YOU: _____.

OPERATOR: What's your home phone number?

YOU: _____.

OPERATOR: What is your name and address?

YOU: _____.

OPERATOR: Please spell your name.

YOU: _____.

OPERATOR: Is anyone at that number now?

YOU: _____.

OPERATOR: I'll connect your call. Please hold.

YOU: _____.

2 Talking on the Telephone

Sometimes we have problems with the telephone. We get the wrong number, someone calls us by mistake, or someone has trouble understanding what the other person is saying. All these situations require telephone courtesy and understanding.

Model Dialogues

Practice these model conversations with a partner.

1. You accidentally dial the wrong number.

PERSON: Hello.

YOU: May I speak with Dr. McGuire?

PERSON: You have the wrong number.

YOU: I do?

PERSON: What number did you dial?

YOU: 239-8063.

PERSON: This is 239-8064. Try it again.

YOU: I'm sorry to have bothered you.

PERSON: That's okay. Good-bye.

2. Someone dials your number by mistake.

YOU: Hello.

PERSON: Is Terry there?

YOU: There is no one here by that name.

PERSON: Are you sure?

YOU: Yes, I'm sure. You have the wrong number.

PERSON: Is this 645-9234?

YOU: No, it isn't.

PERSON: I'm terribly sorry.

YOU: That's okay. Good-bye.

3. You have just dialed the wrong number. It was a long-distance call, and you don't want to be charged for your mistake.

OPERATOR: This is the operator. May I help you?

YOU: Yes, I dialed (716) 433-6947 and got the wrong number.

OPERATOR: I'm sorry. Do you know what number you reached?

YOU: No, I don't.

OPERATOR: What is your number?

YOU: (212) 789-4982.

OPERATOR: I'll credit your account and place the call for you.

YOU: Thank you.

Quick Customs Quiz

Below are situations in which you might find yourself in the United States or Canada. Read each situation, decide what is appropriate, and choose the answer that best fits the circumstance. Draw a circle around the letter in front of your answer. Check your answers against those on page 183, which are the answers an American or a Canadian would probably give. Then discuss with your classmates how you would handle these situations in your country. (If more than one answer is possible, circle all that apply.)

1. The telephone company sent you a bill, which you paid. Now you have received a letter saying you never paid the bill. What should you do?

    a. Nothing. You know you've paid.
    b. Call them and explain the situation.
    c. Find proof that you've paid them (canceled check or receipt), copy it, and send it to the telephone company.

2. When you answer the telephone, the caller asks for someone who does not live there. Obviously, the caller has the wrong number. What should you do?

    a. Hang up.
    b. Begin a conversation.
    c. Tell the caller he or she has reached a wrong number.
    d. Tell the caller your number and ask what number he or she dialed.

147

3. You have made a long-distance call, which you've dialed directly. Unfortunately, you dialed the wrong number and were connected with someone in another state. What should you do?

    a. Nothing.
    b. Call the operator and explain your mistake.
    c. Refuse to pay for the call when you get your bill.
    d. Dial again and hope you get the party you wanted.
    e. Check the phone number and make sure you have written it down correctly.

4. You have called a place of business. The receptionist answers, "Stephans Air Conditioning. Please hold." Then you hear a click and silence. What should you do?

    a. Hang up.
    b. Yell into the phone, "Hello, hello, is anyone there?"
    c. Keep the phone to your ear and wait.
    d. Hang up and call back.

5. You are talking on the phone with someone, and all of a sudden there is silence. The other person is not there any longer. What should you do?

    a. Hang up. He or she obviously didn't want to talk with you any more and hung up.
    b. Hang up and call back. Obviously, something went wrong with the telephone.
    c. Hang on until the connection is restored.

6. Someone calls your house, says obscene words, and tries to talk to you. What should you do?

    a. Hang up.
    b. Yell at the person.
    c. Talk to the person.
    d. Ask the person's name.
    e. Tell the person your name.
    f. Call the phone company and complain.

7. You have called an airline, and someone has said, "Hello, Flight Time Airline. No one is available now to take your call. Please stay on the line until the next available attendant can help you." You hear a click, and music begins to play. What should you do?

    a. Hang up.
    b. Hold the line and wait.
    c. Call the airline later.
    d. Call the operator because there is trouble with the phone.

8. You have called a plumber because you have a leaky faucet. When you call, you hear the following taped message; "Hello, this is Joe the Plumber. I'm not here now. At the sound of the tone, please leave your name, phone number, and the nature of the problem. I'll contact you as soon as I can." Then you hear a beep. What should you do?

    a. Hang up.
    b. Hold the line and wait.
    c. State your name, phone number, and the problem you're having. Then hang up.
    d. Ask him to repeat what he said.
    e. Tell him that you don't speak English very well and that he should speak more slowly.

9. You call the operator from a friend's house and ask to have the call you are about to make charged to your home phone number. What do you expect the operator to do?

   a. Bill the person you are calling for the call.
   b. Bill you at your home phone number for the cost of the call, but only if someone is at your house to accept the charges.
   c. Bill the call to the number from which you are calling.

10. When you answer the phone, you hear, "Hello, this is the operator. I have a collect call for anyone from Ralph Cummings. Will you accept the charges?" What should you do?

    a. Say yes if you wish to pay for the call from Ralph Cummings.
    b. Say no if you do not wish to pay for the call or if you do not know the person making the call.
    c. Ask the operator why he or she has called.

11. You make a phone call. When the ringing stops you hear, "The number you have dialed has been temporarily disconnected. This is a recording." What should you do?

    a. Ask the person to repeat the message.
    b. Say, "What? I don't understand."
    c. Hang up, check the number in the phone book, and dial again.

12. You have called an operator for assistance in making a long-distance call. The operator tells you, "You can dial that direct." What should you do?

    a. Hang up and dial the number yourself.
    b. Ask the operator to help you.
    c. Hang up and call the operator back.

Let's Share   Share with your classmates an interesting experience you have had while using the telephone in your country and in the United States or Canada. Then tell your classmates what is different about using or owning telephones in your country.

3   Business and Social Uses of the Telephone

Telephones play an interesting role in life in the United States and Canada. In addition to being used for business purposes and to relay information, they are used to socialize. North Americans who find themselves separated by distance from family and friends call to keep in touch. They telephone family members on birthdays and holidays if they cannot visit. In most families, the members who use the telephone the most are teenagers who call friends after school. Sometimes parents buy a second phone for their children to use.

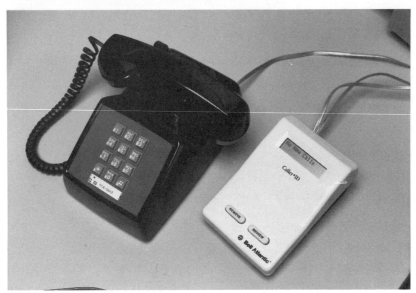

Let's Share Discuss the following questions with your classmates.

1. Who uses the phone most in your family?
2. Do people have several telephones in their homes in your country?
3. Do people talk on the telephone instead of visiting each other?
4. Look at the photos above, of North Americans using the telephone. Do these photos reflect how people in your country use the telephone?

Idioms And Phrases

Let's consider some phrases that are commonly used in telephone conversations. Study them carefully, and use them in the conversation sections here, as well as when you use the telephone in real life.

1. RECEPTIONIST: Will you hold?

    CALLER: Yes.

2. RECEPTIONIST: (*formal*) May I tell Dr. Smith who is calling?

    CALLER: Certainly. This is Jim Jones.

3. RECEPTIONIST: (*informal*) Who's calling? Who is this?

    CALLER: Jim Jones.

4. OTHER PERSON: Whom do you wish to speak to? *or* To whom do you wish to speak?

   CALLER: I would like to speak to Aimee Cummings.

   OTHER PERSON: She isn't here right now. Can I take a message?

   CALLER: (*formal*) Yes, please ask her to return my call at 654-9234.
   (*informal*) Please have her call me back at 654-9234.

Model Dialogues   Read and study these dialogues.

1. OTHER PERSON: You have the wrong number.

   CALLER: I'm sorry. (*hangs up*)

2. CALLER: Hello, may I speak with José García?

   OTHER PERSON: I'm sorry. You have the wrong number.

   CALLER: Is this 234-9874?

   OTHER PERSON: No. I'm sorry. Good-bye.

3. OTHER PERSON: Hello. This is Joe's Pizza. Can I help you?

   CALLER: Yes. I'd like a large cheese and sausage pizza.

   OTHER PERSON: Do you want anything else?

   CALLER: Yes, I'd like four mixed salads and four ginger ales.

   OTHER PERSON: What is your address?

   CALLER: I live at 435 Melville Street.

   OTHER PERSON: That comes to ten thirty-four. We'll deliver your order in about twenty-five minutes.

   CALLER: Thanks. I'll be looking for you.

4. CALLER: Hello. This is Anna Joseph. May I please speak with Elise Eisenburg?

   OTHER PERSON: I'm sorry, but she's not here now. Can I take a message?

   CALLER: Yes. Please tell her I called to ask her about the math homework. Ask her to call me this evening at 654-9234.

   OTHER PERSON: Okay. I'll tell her as soon as she gets home.

   CALLER: Thank you. Good-bye.

   OTHER PERSON: 'Bye.

4   Using the Directory

The telephone directory, or phone book, is an alphabetical listing of the names, addresses, and phone numbers of all the people in an area who have phones and want their number to be listed. There is no charge to have your telephone number listed in the phone book, but some people prefer not to have their number listed. When a phone number is **unlisted**, you can't find it in the directory or get it from the operator.

It's important to know how to use the telephone directory. The directory has white pages that list the names of people and businesses that have phones. The yellow pages, in the back of the directory or in a separate book, list the names and numbers of businesses. They also have advertisements for some of the businesses listed. The yellow pages are classified alphabetically by **subject.** You can find a listing of plumbers, electricians, physicians, schools, and so on. Under each heading is an alphabetical listing of all the local businesses or people in that category.

White Pages

Gable, S. 321	Walton Av	225-3396
Garrod, Albert	1426 Mape Dr	446-5891
Gasten, Mark	686 Elmwood Av	454-6381
Gasten, Henry	687 Elmwood Av	454-6197
Geller, Nancy	459 Titus	645-6216
Glent, R.C.	566 Elm	425-7824
Gold, Seymour	455 Main	334-5872
Hallanhan, N.	366 Finn	746-0351
Holiday, Norman & Mary	263 Court	569-9023

Yellow Pages

RESTAURANTS

Mama's Pizzeria	425 Alexander	422-6891
Ming Hua	3982 Main	587-0034
Mindy's Salad Bowl	364 Elm Av	468-2342
Myron's Deli	2651 Ridge	536-8974
Northeast Inn	126 Lake Av	587-7772
O'Grady's	222 Sport	468-2399

Here is the kind of emergency information you would find in a telephone directory:

Basic Emergency Numbers

Ambulance Service	437-9804
Fire Department	433-8901
Police Department	232-5870
Poison Control	534-0624
Any Emergency	911 (special number used in some areas to contact help in any emergency)

Important: The numbers listed above are not real. You must look up the correct emergency phone numbers for the town or city you are in. They are different in each area of the United States and Canada.

The front of the phone book contains the phone numbers that may be needed in emergency situations. Before we continue, please look up these phone numbers for your city, and write them down in the space provided.

Police Department: _____

Fire Department: _____

Poison Control: _____

Ambulance Service: _____

For long-distance calls, you must dial either 1 or 0. Use one (1) if you call from a home telephone, zero (0) if you call from a pay telephone or need the operator to assist you, as with a collect call. Next dial the three-digit area code for that city, then the person's seven-digit telephone number. If you need a phone number for someone who lives in another state or area code, dial 1, the appropriate area code, and then 555-1212.

Here are the area codes of some parts of the United States and Canada. If you are calling a number in another country, dial 011 plus the country, code, city code, and the number.

United States

California
  Los Angeles 213
  San Francisco 415
Colorado
  Denver 303
District of Columbia 202
Florida
  Miami 305
  Orlando 407
Michigan
  Detroit 313
New York
  Albany 518
  New York City
    Bronx, Manhattan 212
    Brooklyn, Queens,
    Staten Island 718
  Rochester 716

Pennsylvania
  Pittsburgh 412
  Philadelphia 215
South Carolina 803
Texas
  Dallas 214
  Forth Worth 817
  Houston 713

Canada

Alberta 403
Ontario
  Ottawa 613
  Toronto 416
Quebec
  Montreal 514
  Quebec City 418

5 Exploring North America

The front of the phone book provides information about making calls, such as when rates are lowest and what numbers to call to get directory assistance (information) in various parts of the country. Here are some activities that will help you to become familiar with the phone book.

1. Look in the phone book and write down the area code you would dial to reach the directory-assistance operator in each of the following cities.

United States

New York, New York
  1 (   ) 555-1212

Canada

Toronto, Ontario
  1 (   ) 555-1212

Los Angeles, California
1 (   ) 555-1212
Forth Worth, Texas
1 (   ) 555-1212
Seattle, Washington
1 (   ) 555-1212
Denver, Colorado
1 (   ) 555-1212

Quebec City, Quebec
1 (   ) 555-1212
Vancouver, British Columbia
1 (   ) 555-1212

2. Find the chart in the front of the phone book that lists the telephone rates at different times of the day.

   When are the rates the lowest? _____

   When are the rates the highest? _____

   Look up the rates for calling each of the cities listed in number 1 above. Write down the lowest rates.

   _____   _____

   _____   _____

   _____   _____

   _____   _____

   _____   _____

   _____   _____

   _____   _____

3. Now use the directory to look up and write down the phone numbers of the following:

   Department of Motor Vehicles _____

   Immigration and Naturalization Services _____

   Main branch of the public library _____

4. Using the yellow pages of the directory, find a phone number for each of the following:

   A florist: _____

   A TV repair service: _____

   A dentist: _____

   A pizza parlor: _____

An airline: _____

5. Look up the name *Smith*. How many are listed? _____

Analysis: Names

Smith is a very common name in the United States and Canada.

The names listed in U.S. and Canadian phone directories represent the countries all over the world that North Americans come from. Here is a listing of some names. Can you identify the probable ethnic background of each person listed? The answers are on page 184.

Timothy O'Donnell: _____

Rachel Rosenberg: _____

Ahmed Hussain: _____

Anthony Demarco: _____

Ming Hua Huang: _____

Demitrios Kostopoulos: _____

Pedro Fuentes: _____

Huynh Nguyen: _____

Fritz Mann: _____

Vladimir Shostov: _____

While the United States has in the past been called a giant "melting pot," Canada prefers to be considered a "cultural mosaic." Both countries are home to people from many different cultural and religious backgrounds.

Let's Share

Here are some exercises about names.

1. Do the names in your culture tell you something about people or their families? If you answer yes, write some names on the lines below and explain what a native of your country would know about the person upon learning his or her name.

_____

_____

_____

2. Write down a name that is very common in your language. Look it up in the local phone book. Write down the number of people with that name living in

   your city. _____

3. In the United States and Canada, what does Jr. or III after a man's name mean?

Telephone Practice

Here are some tasks to give you more practice using the telephone. If you are in an English-speaking country, use an actual telephone to complete the task. If you are not, role-play these tasks with your instructor.

1. Call two airlines and ask them for the rate of a round-trip ticket to your favorite country. Explain that you want the cheapest flight, non-stop if possible.
2. Call the library and ask if it has books or records in your native language.
3. Call a local theater or concert hall and ask what is playing and the times. If possible, request a brochure on future events this season.
4. Call a florist and ask the cost of sending flowers to someone in a city where you have relatives or friends.
5. Call a stadium and ask what game is going to be played there this weekend.
6. Look up a movie in the newspaper. Call the theater and listen to the recorded message. Write down the information.

Role-Play Most of the time when you answer the telephone, you do not know who is calling or what they are going to say. In this exercise, you will have the freedom to decide the purpose of the call and to respond to the spontaneous conversation of your partner.

For example, if you call a doctor, you must decide on the purpose of your call. You might call to do any of these things:

Make an appointment
Ask what to do because you are sick
Cancel an appointment
Get the result of a blood test or a throat culture
Ask about your bill (U.S. only)

The person you call, in this case a partner from class, will answer the phone and respond to what you say. However, your partner's response may not always be what you expect. For example, if you say, "This is Tanya Askanowski, and I want to make an appointment," your partner might say, "Who? Please spell your name," or "Sorry, you have the wrong number," or "What is the appointment for?" Each of you must respond to what the other says. Practice using the example just given. Choose a partner. Decide who will make the phone call and who will answer the phone. Then begin the role-play with a call to the doctor.

Optional Activity: If a tape recorder is available, your teacher may want to tape some of the conversations. Later, the teacher may play the tapes back to the class, where you can discuss their content, the appropriateness of the students' responses, the students' grammar, and how comfortable the participants were speaking spontaneously. Using the rating sheet on page 157 for this activity.

Your teacher may also choose to have you work in a group of four instead of in pairs. Two people can role-play while the other two observe. Observers should use the rating sheet on page 157.

Exercise

With a different partner, role-play each of the following calls. You may use one of the purposes given for the call or make up one of your own.

1. Call a friend

> to chat.
> to get the homework for one of your classes.
> to get someone's phone number.
> to make plans to go out.
> to extend an invitation to a party or social event.
>
> to _____.

2. Call a relative

   to chat.
   to wish him or her a happy birthday.
   to find out if his or her cold or other illness is better.
   to invite the family to dinner.

   to _____.

3. Call the library

   to find out what time they open and close.
   to find out if they have a particular book.
   to find out how to get a library card.
   to ask what the fines are for late books.

   to _____.

4. Call a classmate

   to ask when a test will be given.
   to ask for help with schoolwork.
   to ask if tomorrow is a holiday.

   to _____.

Conversation Rating Sheet

Circle the number that indicates how well you feel the conversational pair communicated. The lowest rating is 1, the highest 5.

1. The conversation was easy to understand.
   Not easy   1   2   3   4   5   Very easy
2. Their responses to each other were appropriate.
   Not appropriate   1   2   3   4   5   Very appropriate
3. The participants seemed comfortable talking to each other.
   Uncomfortable   1   2   3   4   5   Very comfortable
4. The English they used was correct.
   Incorrect   1   2   3   4   5   Correct
5. They used appropriate idioms and phrases.
   Inappropriate   1   2   3   4   5   Appropriate

6 Special Uses of the Telephone

Using 800 and 900 Numbers

As a convenience to the consumer, many businesses and agencies provide a special number so that their customers may call them long distance free of charge. This is called an **800 number**. To use an 800 number, dial 1-800 and then the seven-digit phonenumber of the company. If you don't know if the company you want to reach long distance has an 800 number, dial 0, and ask the operator for the 800-number operator. This operator can give you the 800 number for any company, hotel, or agency which has one in the United States.

Here is an example of an advertisement that includes an 800 number. What is the company selling? Why do you think they provide a free long-distance number? What audience are they trying to reach?

Other numbers, called **900 numbers,** are not free. These numbers, which may cost as much as $5.00 per minute to call, are used to sell many products and services, from information about jobs to hints on how to maintain your car. Many of the 900 numbers are legitimate businesses that want the caller to pay the cost of the call. However, other numbers are designed to take advantage of the caller by charging very high rates or encouraging unauthorized callers, such as children, to call. Some numbers even provide a person who will have suggestive sexual conversations with the caller.

Here are some advertisements that contain 900 numbers. What are the advertisers

selling? How much will it cost to call each number?

When calling a 900 number, you need to find out how much the call will cost before you dial. In most states, the caller must be informed at the start of the call or in the advertisement about the charges for using the 900 number. If you don't want anyone to be able to dial 900 numbers from your telephone, you can ask your local phone company to block access to 900 numbers from your phone.

Telephone and Computerized Surveys

Some companies will have a representative call to sell you their product or service. Sometimes, they will even use a computer to make the sales call. In either case, if you are not interested, politely say so and hang up.

Various legitimate organizations may call to take surveys about anything from household products to how your spent you vacation. They ask questions so that they can plan their advertising campaigns or design products that consumers will buy. Some will ask personal questions. You are not under any obligation to participate in telephone surveys. If you are not interested in participating, say so politely and hang up.

Unscrupulous individuals, called "con artists," sometimes call and pretend they are taking a survey. During the survey, they will ask you personal questions about when and where you work, about your credit cards, or about your home. Sometimes, they will offer a deal that is "too good to be true," for example, an airline ticket to Japan for $200.

To get the ticket, they will ask you to send a money order or check or to give the number of your credit card. Chances are, you will never get the ticket, but they will get your money.

Before you buy from a telephone solicitor, call the Better Business Bureau (listed in the phone book) and ask questions about the company. If the salesperson tells you that you must make up your mind "right now or you will lose your chance," say, "No, thank you." If you decide to buy the product, get complete information so that you can contact the company if you are not satisfied with the product.

Using Fax Numbers

Fax numbers are used to send documents by modum from location to location. Most government offices and many businesses have fax numbers so that they can receive and send communications, documents, and even photographs almost instantly from one location to another.

To use a fax number, you must first find a fax sending point. Many businesses, such as convenience stores and supermarkets, have fax machines that you may use to send documents to a fax number. If you do not know how to use the machine, ask someone to help you.

Here is an advertisement of a business that has a fax number. What kinds of documents do you think this business would send and receive? What advantage do you think having a fax number gives a business?

7 Summary

Exploring North America

Complete each activity and then share your findings in class.

A. As you watch television, make note of the 800 and 900 numbers that appear. Note the number, the products being sold, and the cost of the call. Discuss your findings with the class.

B. Choose a well-known product or company. Call the 800-number operator to get the 800 number for that company.

C. Call your local telephone company to find out what you must do and how much you must pay to keep people from dialing 900 numbers from your telephone.

D. Call the phone company and ask what special services they have, such as call waiting and call forwarding. Be prepared to explain these services to your class.

Speaking Out   Read each question and be prepared to discuss the issues in class.

A. Many 900 numbers are used to provide the caller with the opportunity to listen to lewd sexual conversations. The charges for calls to these numbers are very high, and there is no restriction on who may call. Some teenagers and preteens call these numbers on their parents' phones. Sometimes, charges for these calls can add up to hundreds of dollars before the parents find out about the calls. Although the parents didn't authorize the calls, they still must pay the bill.

1. Should individuals be allowed to set up 900 numbers that offer obscene conversations? Why or why not?
2. Should the parent or owner of the phone be responsible for 900-number calls that he or she didn't make or authorize? Why or why not?
3. What restrictions do you think should be put on those who offer products and services on 900 numbers?

B. Soon, technology that enables us to see the person we are talking with will be available. Would you want a "video phone"? What are the advantages and disadvantages of having a "video phone"?

C. Should companies be allowed to use computers to sell products and services to customers over the telephone? Why or why not? What do you think about computer-generated sales?

What's Going On Here?   Read about Ellen's experience with the Burns family. Then, with your classmates, answer the *Discussion Questions* that follow.

Ellen went to Canada for the summer as an exchange student. She lived in a house withMr. and Mrs. Burns and their three children. From the very beginning, she was made to feel at home. They told her that their house was her house: She should feel free to live in their house as if it were her own. She called Mr. and Mrs. Burns "Mom" and "Dad," and she felt as though she had three Canadian siblings.

Ellen could invite friends home from school; she could go to the refrigerator whenever she wanted, use the telephone whenever she wanted, and even drive the family car! She was very happy.

After she had been with the Burns family for about a month, Ellen came home from school to find Mr. and Mrs. Burns looking very upset. Mrs. Burns was looking at the telephone bill, and when Ellen came into the house she said, "Ellen, you seem to have made many phone calls home."

"Yes," Ellen replied. "I call my mother every week. It's so nice of you to treat me like your very own children, with freedom to use the telephone and the car. You are really wonderful people."

Mrs. Burns said, "Yes, of course, Ellen, we have tried very hard to make you feel like part of the family. But this month we received a telephone bill for $350! Most of it is for calls to your country. That's a lot of money, and we can't be expected to pay for these calls."

"I'm sorry," Ellen said. "I guess I misunderstood." She left the room in tears.

Discussion questions

1. What is the misunderstanding?
2. Do Mr. and Mrs. Burns expect Ellen to pay for these calls? Should Ellen repay them? What should she do if she doesn't have $350?
3. How did this misunderstanding happen?
4. Who is at fault?
5. How could this situation have been avoided?

Nine

Going to the Doctor

In some countries, such as Canada, medical care is free. All immigrants and refugees have a health card with a number on it; they present the card when they enter a health facility. People may visit the doctor, go to the hospital for surgery or tests, without paying. Students and visitors on visas would have to pay for health care. In the United States, however, health care is very expensive. A visit to the doctor may cost from $25 to $250. Hospital care can cost more than $200 a day. Because health care is so expensive, most people have health insurance. In this way, they pay a flat fee for individual or family coverage. The insurance company then pays all or part of their medical bills. What system of health care exists in your country? How does it work?

In this chapter, we will practice typical conversations that patients have while setting up appointments and when actually visiting the doctor's office. We will also discuss culture shock, and its symptoms, which may appear when people move to a new culture.

1 Preparing for a Visit to the Doctor

Choosing a Doctor

If you don't have a family doctor, you should find one now, while you're healthy. The best way to find a good doctor is to ask friends to recommend one to you. Then call the doctor and make an appointment for a checkup. However, if no one can recommend a physician to you in the United States, call the American Medical Association in your area and ask them to recommend a local doctor. The AMA is listed in the telephone directory. In Canada, contact the local provincial Medical Association (such as the Ontario Medical Association, in Ontario).

Now You Do It

With a partner, complete the following dialogue, in which you ask a friend to recommend a doctor to you. When you have finished, role-play your dialogue with another classmate.

YOU: _____?

FRIEND: Well, I go to Dr. Susan Goddard. But across the street from your apartment building is a new doctor, Dr. Tai Lee. I've heard he is very good, also.

YOU: _____?

FRIEND: I'm not sure about the telephone number, but you can find it in the yellow pages of the telephone book under "physicians."

YOU: _____.

Now write a dialogue in which you call the American Medical Association (AMA) and ask them to recommend a physician.

AMA: Hello. American Medical Association. Can I help you?

YOU: _____.

AMA: What kind of doctor are you looking for? A general practitioner or a specialist?

YOU: _____?

AMA: A general practitioner (sometimes called a primary-care physician) treats a variety of illnesses and will treat your whole family. A specialist concentrates in one area, like cardiology or dermatology.

YOU: _____.

AMA: In that case, you may want to call Dr. Thomas McGee at 555-9874 or Dr. Roseanna Prater at 555-5370.

YOU: _____.

AMA: If we can help you, pleae call again. Good-bye.

Put these conversations into practice by finding out the name of a doctor near where you live and writing his or her name, address, and phone number below. (If you already have a doctor, write his or her name, address, and phone number below). When you get home, write this information near your telephone.

Doctor's name: _____

Address: _____

Telephone number: _____

Matching: Specialists There are many different kinds of doctors, each specializing in a particular area of medicine. Can you match the doctor in the left-hand column with the area in which the doctor specializes in the right-hand column? Answers are on page 184.

_D_ 1. Chiropodist

_E_ 2. Pediatrician

_L_ 3. Gynecologist

_M_ 4. Obstetrician

_A_ 5. Neurologist

_H_ 6. Urologist

_C_ 7. Orthodontist

_B_ 8. Dentist

_G_ 9. Veterinarian

_N_ 10. Anesthesiologist

_I_ 11. General practitioner (GP)

_J_ 12. Internist

_O_ 13. Orthopedist

_K_ 14. Plastic surgeon

_F_ 15. Ophthalmologist

A. A doctor who treats problems related to the nerves

B. A doctor who cares for teeth

C. A dentist who straightens teeth

D. A doctor who takes care of feet

E. A doctor who treats children only

F. A doctor who treats eye problems

G. A doctor who treats animals only

H. A doctor who treats urinary-tract problems

I. A doctor who treats the entire family and who does not specialize in only one area

J. A doctor who specializes in internal medicine

K. A doctor who performs cosmetic surgery

L. A doctor who treats women's problems

M. A doctor who cares for pregnant women

N. A doctor who puts patients to sleep prior to surgery

O. A doctor who treats bone problems

Idioms and Expressions   It is important to be able to describe to the doctor the problem you are having. To be accurate, you need to know the correct terminology. The crossword puzzle on the next page consists of terms often used to describe illness. See how many you know. The answers are on page 184.

Across

1. A tightened muscle that causes pain
3. To cause pain by overstraining a joint
5. Pain in the belly
8. Causes pain on swallowing
11. Pain in the head
12. To throw up
13. Out of place (bone)
16. Feeling that the room is spinning
17. High body temperature
19. Illness caused by an influenza virus

Down

1. Unable to move one's bowels
2. Cracked or split (bone)
4. Pain in the ear
6. Feeling as if you want to throw up
7. Hazy (vision)
9. Hole in a tooth
10. Loose and frequent bowel movements
14. Puffed up
15. Particular sensitivity to certain foods or medicines
18. Redness covering a portion of the skin
20. Pertaining to the nose

Model Dialogues

Practice these dialogues with a classmate.

1. PERSON A: What's the matter? I heard you were sick.

   PERSON B: I feel awful. I have a headache, fever, and diarrhea.

   A: Do you feel dizzy?

   B: Yes, I'm dizzy, too.

2. A: What happened to your knee? It looks swollen.

   B: I had an accident. I fell down the stairs.

3. A: Your eyes look puffy, and you sound nasal.

   B: I'm allergic to cats

Let's Share

Every culture has "home remedies" for ailments and also superstitions about how to keep illness away. What do people in your culture do to alleviate suffering from these common illnesses? When you have finished, share your remedies with the class. Fill in the last column of the chart.

Illness	In the United States/Canada	In Your Country
1. Cold	Take aspirin, lots of fluids, vitamin C; rest and keep warm.	
2. Flu	Take aspirin, liquids, vitamin C; rest and keep warm.	
3. Hiccups	Hold your breath and count to ten; drink a glass of water; or ask someone to scare you.	
4. Headache	Take aspirin and rest.	
5. Diarrhea	Take clear liquids only; eat no solid food except toast or crackers.	
6. Swelling from an injury	Apply cold compresses (ice wrapped in a cloth).	
7. Fever	Take aspirin; take a cool bath.	

Box continued on the following page

Box continued from the preceding page

Illness	In the United States/Canada	In Your Country
8. Mosquito bites	Apply cool compresses.	

Photo Essay   What is happening in each of these photographs? Answers are on page 185.

1.

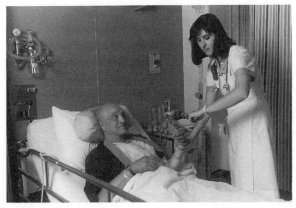

2.

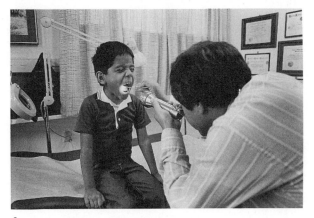

3.

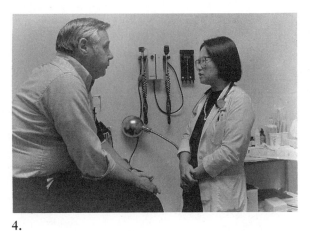

4.

Quick Customs Quiz   Below are situations in which you might find yourself in North America. Read each situation, decide what is appropriate, and choose the answer that best fits the circumstance. Draw a circle around the letter in front of your answer. Check your answers against those on page 185, which are the answers a North American would probably give. (If more than one answer is possible, circle all that apply.)

1. You are walking outside with some friends and step on a rusty nail. What should you do?

   a. Continue walking.
   b. Wash the wound and put a bandage on it.
   c. Call the doctor and ask if you need a tetanus shot.

2. You are in school, and your teacher has sent you to the school nurse because your eyes are red. The nurse thinks you have "pink eye" (conjunctivitis) and calls your parent or guardian to take you home. What should you do?

   a. Rest that afternoon and then return to school.
   b. Go to the doctor.

3. You have a sore throat that has lasted for two weeks. What should you do?

   a. Go to the drugstore and ask for medicine.
   b. Gargle with salt water.
   c. Ignore it and it will go away.
   d. Go to the doctor.

4. The doctor puts you on penicillin and tells you to finish the medicine, which should last ten days. You feel fine after four days. What should you do?

   a. Take the medicine for ten days as the doctor said.
   b. Stop taking the medicine.
   c. Give the medicine to a friend who seems to have the same problem.

5. You have fallen and think you may have broken your leg. You are in great pain. It is 11:00 P.M. What should you do?

   a. Go to your doctor's house.
   b. Go to your doctor's office.
   c. Call the doctor at home.
   d. Call the doctor at his office.
   e. Go to the emergency room at the nearest hospital.
   f. Wait until morning to call the doctor or go to the doctor's office.

6. The receptionist at the doctor's office gives you a bill for $40 for your office visit. You do not have $40. What should you do?

   a. Take the bill with you and pay later.
   b. Explain that you can't pay the bill.
   c. Tell her it's too expensive and ask her to charge you less.
   d. Go home and find a present to give the doctor instead of cash.
   e. Write a check even though you don't have the money to pay.
   f. Ask the receptionist to put the amount you owe on your charge card.

7. You have not been feeling well and go to see the doctor. During the examination, he asks you some very personal questions about your life; for example, Do you have many friends? Do you go out socially? Do you lose your temper often? What is worrying you? When you are asked such questions, what should you do?

   a. Tell him it's none of his business.
   b. Answer his questions and ask him why he's asking them.
   c. Do not answer his questions.
   d. Respond politely.
   e. Tell him that you only came to him to take care of your physical problems.

8. You have a 3:30 P.M. appointment with the doctor. You arrive at her office at 3:25. It is now 4:15, and you are still sitting in the waiting room. What should you do?

   a. Get up and leave.
   b. Yell at the nurse or receptionist.
   c. Walk into the doctor's office.
   d. Continue to wait.
   e. Ask the receptionist how much longer the doctor will be.
   f. Find another doctor.

9. You have a doctor's appointment at 10:30 A.M. When you arrive, the office is very crowded. What should you do?

    a. Take a seat and wait for the nurse to call you.
    b. Leave because it appears you will have a long wait.
    c. Go up to the receptionist, give her your name, and take a seat.
    d. Come back later.

Idioms and Expressions

Here are some questions that the doctor may ask you when you visit his or her office and some questions that you may wish to ask the doctor.

Things the Doctor May Say to You

How long has this (illness, pain) been bothering you?
How long have you had this (sickness, pain, etc.)?
How long has this (the pain, illness, etc.) been going on? Have you had this problem before? If so, when?

Where does it hurt?
Describe your pain.
Does it hurt when I press here?
What are your symptoms?

How did it (the accident) happen?
How did you hurt yourself?

Are you taking any medicine now?
What kind of medicine are you taking for the problem?
Are you allergic to any medicine?

Do you have insurance?
What kind of insurance do you have?
What is your insurance number?

Things the Doctor May Ask You to Do During the Examination

Say "ah." Stick out your tongue.
Open wide.
Hold your breath. Take a deep breath and hold it. Cough.
Now we're going to prick your finger for a blood sample. Give me your finger.
Breathe in deeply and let your breath out slowly.
Bend backward. Bend forward.

Things You May Say to the Doctor

What do you think is wrong?
What should I do about this (problem or illness)?
When will I be feeling better?
How should I take the medicine?
Is it (the illness) contagious?
Does the medicine have any side effects?
Do I need to come for another visit?
How long should I wait to call you if I don't feel better?

Before you go to see your doctor, it is a good idea to make a list of things you want to ask. That way, you will not forget to ask about something you have on your mind. Make sure that you answer and ask questions as specifically as possible. Be direct so that you can get the answers you need. Don't feel shy about asking the doctor to repeat or to explain what he or she has said.

2 Visiting the Doctor

When patients arrive at the doctor's office, they should give their name to the receptionist, say which doctor they have an appointment to see, and wait in the reception room until their name is called. People usually sit one seat apart if possible and read the magazines provided in the reception room.

Each new patient is usually asked to fill out a Patient Health Form upon his or her first visit to the doctor. This form provides the doctor with information about a patient's past medical history.

Look at the sample health form that follows. Fill it out by supplying the appropriate information. Look up in a dictionary any terms that are unfamiliar to you.

PATIENT HEALTH FORM

Name _____ Telephone (____) _____
                                              area code

Address _____
                            number & street

_____ _____ _____
      city   state   zip code

Person to contact in an emergency:

Name _____

Address _____

Telephone _____

Relationship to you _____

If you are covered by health insurance please indicate:

Name of the insurer _____

Address of insurer _____

Contract number _____

PERSONAL HISTORY: Please check (✔) if you have had any of the following medical problems.

Scarlet fever

Measles

German measles

Mumps

Poliomyelitis

Malaria

Ear, nose, and throat
         trouble

Recurrent diarrhea

Kidney or urinary disease

Frequent headaches

Frequent colds

Hay fever, asthma

Tuberculosis

Back problems

High blood pressure

Tumor, cancer, cyst

Stomach trouble

Dizziness, fainting

Diabetes

Are you allergic to any medicines? If so, what? _____

RECORD OF IMMUNIZATIONS

Please fill in date of latest immunization.

DT (Diptheria, tetanus)   _____

Polio (Sabin oral)   _____

Tuberculosis tests   _____

Measles   _____

Mumps   _____

Rubella (German measles)   _____

Other vaccines   _____ _____ _____

Signature _____ Date _____

Role-Play Pain is hard to describe in your own language and even more difficult to describe in another language. Think about when you have been in pain. You might have had a broken arm, a headache, a backache, a toothache, the flu, a head cold, or a stomachache. How can you describe the pain? Some pain is throbbing, some is stabbing, some is piercing, some is dull. Sometimes how we describe a pain can be very important in helping a doctor identify our problem.

Think of a pain you have had and how it felt. The doctor will want to know where it is, how long it has been hurting, when it started, if it goes away, what it feels like, or what kind of a pain it is. Then role-play a visit to a doctor in which you describe an ailment that is causing you pain.

Now You Do It You have come to see your doctor because you have been feeling tired and generally uninterested in things for several weeks. Practice this dialogue with a classmate.

DOCTOR: Hello, I'm Dr. Phillips.

YOU: _____.

DOCTOR: What seems to be the problem?

YOU: I don't know. I just feel tired all the time. I sleep all day. I'm not interested in studying or being with people.

DOCTOR: How long has this been going on?

YOU: _____.

DOCTOR: Are there any other symptoms?

YOU: I'm just tired.

DOCTOR: Do you have many friends?
YOU: _____.

DOCTOR: Are you worried or upset about anything?

YOU: _____.

DOCTOR: Has anything about your life changed?

YOU: _____.

DOCTOR: How long have you lived in this city?

YOU: _____.

DOCTOR: Hmm. Well, let's check you over. (*a few minutes later*) Well, I don't see anything physically wrong with you. Your heart is strong. Lungs are clear. Your blood pressure is in the normal range.

YOU: Then what do you think is wrong with me?

DOCTOR: Sometimes when people move to a new location, especially a new country, they experience culture shock. Things that were easy to do in their own country, like traveling by bus, going shopping, and talking on the telephone, produce anxiety in a new country. Body language, gestures, idioms, foods, customs, socializing are all different. Becoming accustomed to these new ways is a strain. People experience tiredness from always having to think about how to do the simplest things. Sometimes this culture shock can become serious, and people become very depressed. I suggest that you try to spend some time each week with people from your culture with whom you do not have to worry about how to act.

YOU: But my teachers say to speak English all the time.

DOCTOR: I understand, but right now we need to deal with your symptoms. Talk to people from your country, friends, about some of the "funny" ways we act and about some of the problems you have had. This will help you and them to feel better. Try to get out and do the things you enjoy.

YOU: How long does this usually last?

DOCTOR: Culture shock lasts for a while and then begins to disappear. The length of time varies from person to person. Be prepared to feel it again when you return home to your naive country.

YOU: (*surprised*)_____?

DOCTOR: When people reenter their native country, they again experience a cultural change. They must behave in ways that they have not thought about for a long time. They also find that because they have been away to another country, their friends and relatives treat them differently. Also, things in their city may have changed. This creates a shock to the body, and people may react again by withdrawing and sleeping a lot to get away from the strain. This is called reentry shock.

YOU: _____

DOCTOR: If you aren't feeling better in two or three weeks, please call me.

3 Summary

Read the situations below and determine what went wrong and why.

What's Going On Here?

Read about three international students and their health problems. After each story, answer the *Discussion Questions* with your classmates.

A. Mary had been sick all week. She couldn't eat anything. She felt nauseated mostof the time. Her roommate told her to go to the student health center on their college campus, but Mary was afraid to go. She had some medicine from home which she took three times a day, but it didn't seem to be helping. A friend who came from her country brought her some herbs to put in hot water and drink, but that didn't help either.

Finally, on Friday, Mary agreed to go to the doctor. When she arrived, the nurse was very friendly and asked her to fill out some forms. Then she took Mary's temperature and weighed her.

The doctor seemed to be nice, too. She asked Mary how long she had been sick and to describe her symptoms. The doctor listened intently, then she said, "Do you think you might be pregnant?" Mary turned red and didn't answer. She looked down at the floor. She thought to herself, "If I had my clothes on now, I would run out of the office."

During the rest of the visit, Mary didn't look at the doctor or hear anything she was saying. Finally, the doctor gave her a piece of paper and told her to take it to the drugstore.

Discussion questions

1. Why didn't Mary want to go to the health center to see the doctor?
2. Why did she become upset and stop talking to the doctor or listening to what she was saying?
3. Why did she want to run out of the office?
4. Why did the doctor ask Mary if she might be pregnant?

B. Jason had a temperature of 102. His head was stuffed; his bones ached and histhroat was very sore. He knew he had the flu. All his friends had been sick with it. He had used up all the special creams and herbs that his mother had carefully packed and put in his suitcase, saying, "Just in case you get sick."

After three days of lying in bed, feeling miserable, Jason decided to go to the doctor. He described all his symptoms and was sure the doctor would give him a shot that would make him feel much better. Instead, she told him to get plenty of rest and to drink lots of liquids. She gave him a prescription to fill and said that in two or three days he would be feeling better.

As he left, the receptionist told him that his visit would cost $35. Jason paid the money by check and left the doctor's office feeling very angry.

Discussion questions

1. Why was Jason angry?
2. What did he think the doctor would do?
3. What did the doctor tell him to do?

C. Emma didn't ask her family doctor in her home country to fill out the health form that the university had sent her, so when she arrived in the United States, the college gave her a physical exam. They weighed her, took her blood pressure, checked her eyes, gave her a patch test for TB (tuberculosis), and asked her if she had ever had diseases such as chicken pox, mumps, or measles. She said that she had had the chicken pox when she was eight years old, and that she had had a vaccination against the measles. She gave the doctor a piece of paper with the date on which she had the vaccination.

The doctor said that she would need to be vaccinated for measles again. Emma was upset because she had already had a shot. The doctor explained that in the United States you need to have two shots, and they couldn't accept the one she had already had. Emma said that she didn't want to have the shots. The doctor then told her that it was the law that all students receive two measles shots, and that if she refused to be innoculated, she would not be able to stay at school. Emma was very surprised, but she agreed to have the two injections.

A few days later, Emma returned to the college health center for the results of her TB patch test. The doctor told her that the text was positive. Emma said, "That's good," and she got up to leave.

The doctor said, "No, Emma, it's not good. When the test is positive, it means you have the presence of the TB bacillus in your body. That is not good, and we will have to report you to the health department, give you a chest x-ray, and put you on special medication."

Emma was shocked. She said, "I don't have TB. I have been innoculated against it. That's why the test is positive. It's supposed to be that way."

Discussion questions

1. What are the two cultural misunderstandings that occurred in this situation?
2. Why did each of them occur?

Exploring North America

Investigate North American culture by interviewing people, doing research, and hearing as much as you can about the subject presented.

A. When you visit the doctor in Canada or the United States, he or she might prescribe medicine for you to take which you must buy at a pharmacy. Usually, the doctor will prescribe a "brand name" medicine, but he or she may also give you the name of a "generic" drug that you can use instead. The generic drug contains the same ingredients as the brand-name medication, but it costs less. If you want the generic drug, you must tell the pharmacist that you want to buy it instead of the brand-name medicine.

Many over-the-counter (OTC) medicines, which are medicines you can buy without a doctor's prescription, also have generic equivalents. Go to a large pharmacy, department store, or supermarket, and see if you can find generic products with the same ingredients but which cost less than the brand-name items listed here.

Brand name medicine	Generic medicine
1. NYQUIL	_____
2. LISTERINE MOUTH WASH	_____
3. BAYER ASPIRIN	_____

Z4. BAND-AID BANDAGES _____

5. PEPTO BISMOL _____

B. A medical title tells about the kind of education and credentials a person in the health profession has. Find the meaning of each of these terms, and then look in your local telephone book to see if you can find a person with each type of title.

1. Medical Doctor (MD)
2. Chiropractic Physician (DC)
3. Osteopathic Doctor (OD)
4. Doctor of Podiatry (DPM)
5. Dentist (DDS)
6. Registered Physical Therapist (RPT)
7. Registered Nurse (RN)
8. Licensed Practical Nurse (LPN) (U.S.)
9. Registered Nursing Assistant (RNA) (Canada)

C. Go to your college health center or a clinic in your area. Find out what services they offer and who can go to the clinic. Share this information with your class.

Speaking Out   Be prepared to discuss the issues presented.

A. Medical treatment and health insurance in the United States are very expensive. Much of the recent increase in the cost of medical insurance is caused by malpractice suits brought by patients against their doctors. The patient sues the doctor to get a financial settlement, often for millions of dollars, because he or she thinks that the doctor or the hospital provided incompetent care and caused a serious health problem.

1. Do you think that patients should be able to sue doctors and hospitals if they believe their illness was not properly treated? Why or why not?
2. Should limits be set on the amount of money a patient can receive as a settlement in a malpractice suit? How much? Under what circumstances?

B. Currently in the United States, a person who is not covered by a government program such as Medicare or Medicaid must pay his or her own medical and dental bills. People can buy health insurance to help with the costs of medical treatment. However, unless the insurance premiums are paid by the company the person works for, they will cost the person a great deal. The benefits of this system are that Americans may go to any doctor or hospital they choose and do not have to wait to go into the hospital or to have an operation if they need it and can pay for it (or have insurance to cover it).

Because medical insurance and medical treatment are so expensive, many families cannot afford health insurance or the health care they need. Without insurance, however, a serious illness or extended stay in the hospital can cost a family every cent they have; they could even lose their home.

For this reason, some people think that the United States should adopt a government medicine plan similar to those in England, Canada, and Sweden. The plan would provide medical coverage for all families but would spread the cost through additional taxes to all taxpayers.

1. Do you think that government-run medicine is an acceptable way to provide medical coverage? What are the advantages and disadvantages?
2. Does your country have a government-run medical plan? How does it work?
3. Which system do you prefer, socialized medicine or the present American system? Why?

4. Go to the library and learn about President Clinton's health care plan and how it tried to modify the U.S. health care system.

C. In the United States, a physician cannot release a patient's medical records without the patient's permission, except in rare cases, when the public's health would be threatened. This means that parents, schools, or even the police cannot see the patient's records.

1. Do you agree with this policy? Why or why not?
2. In what cases, if any, should a doctor release a patient's records without his or her permission?

Answers

Chapter One

A

B

Analysis   (page 9)

2. At least one seat apart if possible. People read and ignore each other.
3. At least 2 feet apart or more if possible. People do not touch or shove. May look bored or even angry.
4. At least one seat apart if possible. People generally do not speak to other people in a restaurant unless they know them. Hands in lap except when eating.
5. 3 to 4 feet. Erect posture.
6. 2 to 3 feet. Relaxed posture.
7. 3 to 4 feet. Gesture with hands, often use a high-pitched voice, smile, use exaggerated facial gestures.

177

8. 3 to 4 feet unless you know the child well. People do not touch or kiss unless they are members of the family.

(page 16)

Part 1

1. I		6. B	
2. D		7. A	
3. G		8. H	
4. F		9. C	
5. E			

Part 2

10. J		15. M	
11. L		16. P	
12. O		17. Q	
13. K		18. R	
14. N			

Chapter Two

Quick Customs Quiz (page 29)

1. **c.** It is always best to smile and call your teacher by name rather than "teacher."

2. **a.** In North America, it is considered respectful and correct to look directly into the eyes of the person who is talking to you, regardless of that person's position. To look away would seem very impolite to an American and would show that you are not interested or that you lack respect.

3. **a or b.** Depending on the size of the class and the difficulty of the problem, you may either ask for a clarification during the class or see the instructor after class for help.

4. **a.** Call your adviser. Explain your illness and make another appointment for when you are feeling better.

5. **c or d.** Depending on your course requirements and class load, you should either make arrangements with your adviser to drop the class with the instructor's permission or ask the instructor for permission to finish the class work during the next semester.

6. **d.** Attending class, even if the teacher doesn't seem to like you, is very important in North America. Work as hard as you can, and make the most of the class. Speaking to a guidance counselor may help you feel better, but neither the counselor nor your parents can make the teacher change your grade.

7. **a or c.** Class participation is very important in North America. However, if you feel uncomfortable, discuss your feeling with your instructor.

8. **c.** Covering your paper will let the other person know that you do not approve of his cheating. Do not allow anyone to copy your work, because this makes you guilty of cheating too!

9. **c.** Discuss your questions with your teacher privately. Do not ask about the interpretation of grades or answers during the class period.

10. **a.** It is considered correct to volunteer to answer questions. However, do not try to be the one to answer questions all the time. Let other students have the opportunity to answer also.

11. **a or d.** Most teachers are very reasonable and are generally willing to test students at different times if they have a good reason to do so.

Matching: Idioms (page 35)

1. C	5. F	8. E	11. K
2. E	6. J	9. A	12. L
3. J	7. H	10. G	13. D
4. B			

Matching: Model Dialogue (page 38)

A. c, d, a, b   B. b, a, c

Chapter Three

Quick Customs Quiz (pages 50–51)

1. **c.** Politely ask the person to turn down his stereo and give your reasons. If he will not cooperate, then call the housing authorities or the police to make a complaint (**e** or **f**).
2. **b.** Politely but firmly refuse. You don't need to justify your decision or apologize.
3. **b.** You may get into trouble if you allow others to copy your work, and the other person will not learn to work the problems. If someone needs help, you may show them your class notes or teach them to solve the problems, but you should not let them copy your work.
4. **e.** It's generally better to tell someone how you feel and try to work out a solution together before you go to the housing authorities.
5. **a.** Your friend is offering to introduce you and arrange a date for you (fix you up) with someone whom he knows. You do not know the person and therefore are relying on your friend's judgment (blind date). There is no obligation to continue the relationship beyond the first date unless both of you wish to.

Chapter Four

Matching: Idioms and Expressions (pages 61–62)

1. G	5. C	9. A	13. H
2. E	6. I	10. B	14. F
3. K	7. J	11. M	
4. L	8. D	12. N	

Quick Customs Quiz (pages 62–63)

1. **c.** By smiling, you are indicating that you would like to meet him. His smile means that he would like to get to know you and should not be considered bold or rude.
2. **e.** Catching a person's eye and smiling is the best way to show your interest. If the other person wishes to meet you also, he or she will smile back. Actions described in **a, b,** and **c** would be considered shocking or offensive to a North American.
3. **a.** Generally speaking, this phrase is a euphemism for asking a person's consent to have sex. If someone accompanies another person to an apartment or home under these circumstances, he or she is tacitly agreeing to engage in physical intimacy.
4. **a, b, c, d.** These are acceptable forms of public affection; passionate kissing is never acceptable.
5. All of the places listed.

6. **b.** If you are attending a prom, the man should bring the woman a corsage or flowers. The woman may give her date a flower for his buttonhole, usually a rose or carnation to match her dress.

7. **d.** If the man asks the woman out, he should pay the expenses unless they agree to share the expenses before the date. Should the woman ask the man out, she pays for all expenses. The man may pay the tips for dinner or taxis if he wishes, however. If the man or woman are uncomfortable having someone pay for their expenses they may suggest splitting the costs.

8. **b.** Generally speaking, the man picks up the woman at her home unless they agree to meet at another location for the sake of mutual convenience.

Chapter Five

Riddles (page 71)

1. A garbage truck	4. A newspaper
2. A table	5. A pink car-nation
3. A teapot	

Matching (page 78)

1. C	4. B
2. D	5. A
3. E	6. F

Chapter Six

North American Holidays (pages 109–110)

1. Fourth of July	4. Passover
2. Thanksgiving	5. Christmas
3. Easter	

Matching: Greeting Cards (page 110)

1. B	3. A	5. G	7. E
2. C	4. D	6. F	8. H

Matching: Social Events (pages 111–112)

1. H	5. J	9. I	13. A
2. E	6. L	10. G	14. N
3. C	7. K	11. B	15. P
4. M	8. F	12. D	16. O

Quick Customs
Quiz (page 113)

1. **a** or **b**. When an adult is invited to a dinner party, it is considered polite to take a small, relatively inexpensive gift for the hosts, such as a bottle of wine or a box of candy. Unless asked, don't take food. If you are invited to a potluck dinner, however, you should take a dish of food large enough to feed the whole group. The host will usually tell you what type of dish to bring. Don't take a friend or a relative to dinner unless the host has told you that you may do so. Unless children have been specifically invited, do not take them, especially to evening social functions.

2. **a**. Generally speaking, when you are not eating, you should place your hands in your lap, although in very casual situations, you may place your hands and wrists on the table.

3. **b, c, e, g.**

4. **a, e**. Carrying on a conversation is an important part of dining in North America. It is important to let your host know you are enjoying the food by commenting on it verbally, not by burping, smacking your lips, or making any other noises.

5. **b**. The host will ask you if you want a second portion (seconds). If you wish to eat more, thank the host, comment on the food, and take a second helping the first time it is offered. Often the host will ask if you wish to have the last piece of meat or helping from a dish (this is considered polite in North America). If you refuse, the host will assume that you do not want to eat any more and will not ask you again.

   If you are in a very casual situation, such as a picnic or family gathering, you may ask for seconds when yuo want more. Simply say, "Please pass me the (*food*). Thank you."

6. **c**. This is a way to make pleasant conversation but is not necessarily an offer to have dinner. If the offer is ultimately taken up, each person is expected to pay for his or her own dinner.

7. **b**. This is often a pleasantry that people use on parting, not a specific invitation. In the United States or Canada, always call or make arrangements before you go to visit anyone.

8. **c**. The other behaviors would either amuse or irritate other restaurant patrons and your waiter.

9. **a, c, d**. The legal drinking age in the U.S. is between 18 and 21. In Canada it is 18. Since the restaurant or bar must check to see if you are old enough to be served liquor, you must show a piece of identification that has your birth date on it.

10. **a**. sometimes **c** or **e**. Cash is always acceptable and generally preferred. Although more expensive restaurants accept credit cards (Visa, American Express, MasterCard), "family" and "fast food" restaurants like McDonald's, Burger King, and Taco Bell will not. Restaurants will often accept traveler's checks but never personal checks or currencies of other countries.

11. **b**. Tell the waiter that your check is incorrect and ask him to correct it. Because there is an unwritten rule in North America that "the customer is always right," businesses strive to please the customer.

Chapter Seven

Quick Customs
Quiz (pages 134–135)

1. **c**. Americans often browse, and it is perfectly all right to tell the clerk politely that you are just looking.

2. **c**. To receive the discount, you must purchase the product and give the clerk the coupon when you pay for the item. The amount of the coupon will be deducted from your bill.

3. **a** or **d**. Since prices in American stores are fixed, you cannnot bargain for a better price but must pay the amount on the ticket. The only exceptions are articles sold by individuals (used goods) or large articles like automobiles and large appliances.

4. **a** or **c**. The accompanying chart will help you know your size in the United States.

5. **e.** Although you can return a garment if it doesn't fit, you can save yourself a lot of time by trying it on in the fitting room before you buy it. Trying a garment on in the store under or over your clothes or taking it to a rest room to try on could get you arrested for shoplifting (stealing).

6. **a, b, d, e.** All of these are good ideas, especially **e.** The warranty should specifically state what the car dealership will pay for if repairs are needed and how long the car is covered under the terms of the warranty. Ask questions and make sure you understand the terms and the answers.

Clothing Size Conversion Chart

Children's Dresses and Suits

American	2	4	6	8	10	12
European	40–45	50–55	60–65	70–75	80–85	90–95

Women's Clothing

American	6	8	10	12	14	
European	35	38	40	42	44	

Men's Suits and Overcoats

American	36	38	40	42	44	46
European	46	48	50	52	54	56

Women's Shoes

American	4	5	6	7	8	9
European	34	35	36	37	38	39

Men's Shoes

American	7	8	9	10	11	12
European	40	41	42	43	44	45

Men's Shirts

American	14	14½	15	15½	16	16½
European	36	37	38	39	41	42

Quick Customs Quiz

(pages 137–138)

1. **e.** Most stores will not allow returns or refunds after seven days. In this situation, it is best to thank the clerk and leave if you cannot persuade him or her to allow you to return the item.

2. **b.** Most stores will allow you to make an even exchange by letting you substitute an item in a different size or color. They may even allow you to use the purchase price of the item as partial payment for another item. Unless you have a dated sales receipt that shows that the buyer paid cash, you cannot get a cash refund.

3. **b.** New appliances are covered under warranty, which means that the manufacturer will replace or repair the appliance free of charge if anything goes wrong within a stated period of normal use. Keep the warranty and make certain that you understand it.

4. **a.** Unordered merchandise may be kept, but you should notify the company of the error.

5. **c.** It is extremely important that you return the applesauce and jar with the glass to the store so that they may remove from the shelves all the applesauce that was bottled by that company. Otherwise, someone may be injured by eating applesauce with glass in it. In exchange for a product returned under such conditions, the company will replace the product and sometimes give the customer additional packages of the product free.

Chapter Eight

Matching: Telephone Terms

(pages 143–144)

1. M	5. G	9. J	13. D
2. E	6. F	10. H	14. C
3. L	7. I	11. A	15. O
4. B	8. K	12. N	16. P

Quick Customs Quiz

(pages 147–149)

1. **b, then c.** If you feel that a mistake has been made in your bill, you may call the business office and ask them to check your account. If they find no evidence that you have paid, you should either send them or take to them in person proof that you did pay the bill.

2. **c.** When someone dials the wrong number, it is polite to say, "I'm sorry. You have the wrong number." Generally, the person will apologize and hang up. Sometimes people ask for your number. It is better to ask what number they were trying to dial than to give out your number. They generally ask this question to find out how the mistake was made (did they misdal, or is the number they have incorrect?).

3. **b, then e.** If you reach a wrong number on a long-distance call, you should call the operator and explain that you got the wrong number. If you do this, the phone company will not charge you for the call.

4. **c.** The receptionist probably had to answer another call. She has asked you to hold the phone and wait until she can speak with you. This usually only takes a few minutes and is not meant to seem impolite. When she returns to the line, she will probably say, "Thank you for holding. Can I help you?" or "I'm sorry to keep you waiting." If you are in a hurry and cannot wait even a short while, hang up and call back later.

5. **b.** Once in a while, people who are carrying on a conversation get "cut off" (something happens that disconnects their call). If this happens, hang up and either wait for the person to call you back or call the person. (Ordinarily, the person who placed the call in the first place calls again.)

6. **a, later f.** The telephone company suggests that if you get nuisance calls, hang up. Never talk to these people or give them any information. Sometimes they just dial a number at random and don't even know what number they've called. If they continue to phone you, call the phone company and register a complaint.

7. **b.** Airlines, doctor's offices, and other places of business that receive many calls use taped messages to tell people they are busy and ask them to hold the line. To make the caller feel more comfortable and relaxed, they sometimes play music until someone can answer the phone.

8. **c.** More and more places of business and even homes are using tape recorders to play and record phone messages. When you hear a taped message, listen carefully for the message, wait for the beeping sound, and then give your name, telephone number, and any other important information. Be sure to speak slowly and to keep your message short.

9. **b.** The operator will bill your home phone instead of the phone you are using to make the call or the phone whose number you are calling.

10. **a or b.** This is a call in which the person calling tells the operator to charge the call to the people who are receiving the call. The operator always asks the person receiving if he or she will accept the charges (pay for the call). If the reply is no, the call cannot be made.

11. **c.** An operator or tape recording will tell you this if the person you are calling has had the phone disconnected for a while. People sometimes do this when they go on vacation. It can also mean that there are some mechanical problems with the phone or that the telephone company has disconnected the phone.

12. **a.** The operator or a recording will say this to indicate that you do not need help to complete the call (and consequently can avoid paying for the call at the higher, operator-assisted rate).

Irish, Jewish, Arabic, Italian, Chinese, Greek, Hispanic, Vietnamese, German, Russian

Chapter Nine

Matching: (pages 163–164)
Specialists

1. D	5. A	9. G	13. O
2. E	6. H	10. N	14. K
3. L	7. C	11. I	15. F
4. M	8. B	12. J	

Crossword Puzzle   (page 165)
Solution

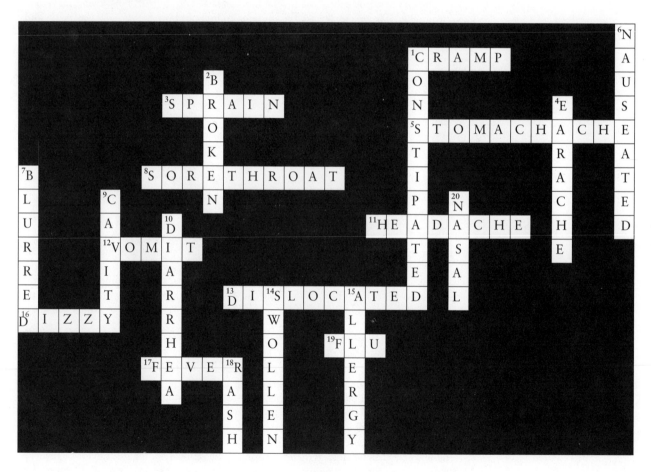

Photo Essay (page 167)

1. waiting room
2. nurse taking a patient's pulse
3. doctor looking at someone's throat
4. patient on an examining table

Quick Customs Quiz (pages 167–169)

1. **b,** then **c.** With a puncture wound, it is best to call a doctor. This type of wound may require a tetanus shot to prevent a more serious illness.
2. **b.** If you are sent home with a contagious illness, either you must wait until you are completely well, as with a sore throat or the flu, or seek medical help to combat the illness.
3. **d.** Most sore throats go away within a few days. A persistent sore throat should be "cultured" for the presence of streptococcus ("strep") infection. Without proper treatment, this can lead to dangerous illness.
4. **a.** Patients should always follow the doctor's directions exactly. If they experience any problems as a result of the medication, they should call the doctor immediately. No prescription medicine should be given to anyone else.
5. **e.** Most doctors' offices are open Monday through Friday from 9 A.M. to 5 P.M. Generally, if you call when the office is closed, a recording will give you a number to call. Call that number and leave a message for the doctor to call you. Patients should not call a doctor at home or go to the doctor's office for assistance when the office is closed. An emergency like a suspected broken leg requires x-rays and immediate attention.
6. **a.** Bills are presented at the time of treatment. Although you are encouraged to pay at this time, you may take the bill with you and mail the payment later. Doctors generally do not accept charge cards.
7. **d.** North American doctors believe that people's life-style and personality have a great deal to do with their physical health. For this reason, doctors ask many questions not only about your health but about your life-style and feelings.
8. **e.** North Americans are accustomed to being kept waiting in a doctor's office. They usually arrive on time, however. If kept waiting for more than a half hour, they politely ask the receptionist how much longer it will be before they see the doctor. When they see the doctor, they may politely mention the long wait by saying, "You must have been very busy today," or "I waited over half an hour to see you." Most doctors try not to keep patients waiting, but it is difficult to know how long a patient's problem may take to diagnose and treat. North American doctors are generally interested in talking with their patients to understand the total problem. (Sometimes a doctor is delayed by an emergency.)
9. **c.** Whenever you go to an office, whether it's a doctor's, dentist's, college, or employment office, you must go up to the receptionist, greet him or her, and give him or her your name. You must do this even though you have an appointment.

Glossary

acquaintance (n)   A person you know or have met. Such people are not usually considered friends because you do not know them well.

He lives next door, I don't know him well. He is just an *acquaintance*.

AIDS (n)   A serious disease, resulting in the loss of the body's immunity to other diseases, which is spread through sexual activity or contact with body fluids such as blood which are infected with the HIV virus.

Because of the rapid spread of AIDS among young people, colleges and government agencies are providing literature and education programs to students about the dangers of AIDS.

all right (adv)   Acceptable, OK, truly.

It is *all right* with me if you finish the test tomorrow.
We will find out the test results tomorrow, *all right!*

American Medical Association (AMA) (n)   The medical association to which most doctors in the United States belong.

Most American doctors are members of the *AMA*.

anniversary (n)   An occasion celebrated to honor each year that people have been married.

A twenty-fifth wedding *anniversary* is called the silver anniversary.

anxiety (n)   Fear or nervousness about something.

anything goes   An expression meaning that any behavior or action is acceptable.

In the 1940s and 1950s, American students often dressed in shirts and ties to go to class. Now *anything goes:* students wear shorts, T-shirts, or even jeans with holes cut out in them to class.

apologize (v)   To say that one is sorry.

People ususally *apologize* when they do something wrong.

baby shower (n)   A party given by the friends or family of a woman who will soon have a baby.

Mary Ann received many presents for the baby at her surprise *baby shower*.

bargain (n)   Something that costs less than it usually should or less than you expected to pay.

I bought this beautiful wool coat for only $50! It is a real *bargain!*

beef patty (n)   A hamburger without the roll.

I just want a *beef patty*. I'm on a diet.

beep (n)   A short, high-pitched sound.

At the sound of the *beep*, please leave your name and message.

blind date (n)   An arrangement, made by a friend, for two people who do not know each other to go out together.

Thomas had a good time on his *blind date*, though he had been hesitant about going.

B.O. (n)   Body odor.

His *body odor* was so strong that people began to leave the room.

body language   (n) Gestures; the movements of the face, hands, and body that add expression to one's speech or reveal one's attitude or feelings about a person or situation.

His *body language*—crossed arms—said that he didn't agree with what the speaker was saying.

bother (n)   An irritation.

Driving to the airport at night is a real *bother*.

bother (v)   To annoy.

The loud music in the next room *bothered* him.

bowling (n)   An indoor game in which people throw a large, heavy ball to knock down ten wooden pins.

Let's go *bowling* this Saturday night.

brand (n)   The specific name given to a manufactured product.

There are many *brands* of shampoo.

bridal shower (n)   A party given by the friends of a woman who is going to be married.

Twenty friends attended June's *bridal shower*.

bride (n)   A woman who is getting married.

Doesn't the *bride* look lovely in her gown!

browse (v)   To look at things in a store without intending to buy anything.

When I was *browsing*, I saw several dresses I would like to buy when I get the money.

buddy (n)   A very good friend; sometimes used ironically to show anger.

This is my *buddy*, Jim, whom I grew up with.
Look, *buddy*, why don't you keep your mouth shut!

cabbie (n)   A person who drives a taxi.

The *cabbie* told him the fare to the airport would be $12.00.

cafeteria (n)   A restaurant in which the customers select food from displays as they pass along a line.

Some people prefer a *cafeteria* because they can see the food and judge the quality of the food before they order it.

catch someone's eye (v)   To look at someone briefly at the same time as that person is looking at you; to get someone's attention.

It took me five minutes to *catch the waiter's eye*.

CD player (n)   A device which plays *compact disk* recordings

A *CD player* will only play compact disk (CD) recordings; it will not play tapes or standard size records.

chapel (n)   A place where people hold religious services, including weddings and funerals.

Funeral services will be in the *chapel* at 4 P.M.

chaperoned date (n)   A date on which an adult accompanies a young couple.

Since their daughter is only 14, her parents insist that she only go on *chaperoned dates*.

checkup (n)   A complete physical examination given when a patient is healthy to be certain that the patient is in good health.

Physicians recommend a yearly *checkup* for everyone over 50.

confide in (someone) (v)   To tell someone something that you would not tell anyone else.

When I had problems with my family, I *confided in* my teacher.

con artist (n)   An unscrupulous individual who takes advantage of the trusting.

Because of their ability to instill trust or to arouse people's greed, *con artists* are able to cheat people out of their life saving by convincing them to invest in fraudulent schemes.

credit card (n)   cards issued by banks or stores which allow the holder to charge merchandise and pay for it later in monthly installments.

Credit cards, like MasterCharge or Visa, are issued by banks to individuals with good credit.

credit (a call) (v)   Not to be charged for a call you have made on the telephone.

The operator *credited* the call because I got the wrong number.

coupon (n)   A certificate issued by a manufacturer which allows the consumer to receive a discount when he purchases a product or service.

The Little Italy Pizza *coupon* allowed the customer to receive a $2.00 discount on the price of a large pepperoni pizza.

culture (n)   1. The society in which one lives.

Each person is a product of his or her native *culture.*

2. The growth and examination, under laboratory conditions, of a sample of bacteria taken from a person's body.

The doctor took a *culture* to see what kind of bacteria were causing his sore throat.

culture shock (n)   A feeling of uneasiness which comes as a result of living in a country where the rules of behavior are different from one's native country.

All people experience *culture shock* to some degree.

dandelion (n)   A plant, usually considered a weed, which has a bright yellow blossom.

While the *dandelion* plant has a lovely yellow flower, most people consider them a pest to have in their yards.

dandruff (n)   Dry flakes of the skin of the scalp that fall from one's hair onto one's shoulders.

He should use a special shampoo to get rid of his *dandruff.*

date (n)   A social, usually romantic occasion spent with someone of the opposite sex.

Do you have a *date* this Saturday night?

date (v)   To go on a date or dates.

I would really like to *date* Terry.
James and Julia have been *dating* for six months.

date rape (n)   When a male forces his date to have sexual intercourse with him against her will during or after a date.

A woman may guard against *date rape* by avoiding situations, such as drinking or passionate embraces, which may lead to loss of control on the male's part.

dating service (n)   An organization that arranges dates for people for a fee.

Some Americans use a *dating service* to help them meet people of the opposite sex.

daydreaming (n)   Not paying attention to what is happening at the time because one is thinking of something else.

The teacher scolded the young boy for *daydreaming* during the math lesson.

deal with (v)   To handle a person or situation.

I had to *deal with* an angry teenager when I said she couldn't go to the rock concert.

demonstration (n)   A gathering of individuals to protest a social, economic, or governmental issue.

The workers organized a *demonstration* to protest against the unsafe working conditions at the processing plant.

deodorant (n)   A product used under the arms to prevent body odor.

Using a *deodorant* is especially important during hot weather.

devil's advocate (n)   One who takes the opposite side in an argument to bring out all points that need to be discussed.

Although he agreed with the Equal Rights Amendment, he played *devil's advocate* by pretending to be against it while asking good questions.

dial (v)   To select the numbers on the telephone.

How do you *dial* a long-distance call?

discount (n)   A reduction in price.

The store was offering a 10 percent *discount* on all children's clothes.

dressy (adj)   Fancy or special (clothes).

Do you think this outfit is *dressy* enough for a wedding?

drive-in (n or adv)   A business where the patron may remain in his car to order food, see a movie, or purchase merchandise.

McDonald's is one of the most popular *drive-in* restaurants in the United States.

dry cleaner (n)   A business which cleans clothes, especially those which cannot be washed with water.

Because I was worried that my new wool coat would shrink if I washed it, I took the coat to the *dry cleaner.*

fall to pieces   An expression meaning to disintegrate.

When I washed the scarf in the washing machine, it *fell to pieces.*

She *fell to pieces* when she heard about the earthquake in her homeland.

farmer's market (n)   A place where farmers sell their fresh fruits, vegetables, and meats to the public. (Also called *public market.*)

It's much cheaper to buy food at the local *farmer's market* than in a supermarket.

fast food (n)   Food such as hamburgers and hot dogs that is available without waiting.

If we eat *fast food,* we can finish lunch quickly and have more time to shop.

feel free (v)   To be comfortable enough in someone's company to do or to say what is on your mind.

When I am at my friend's house, I *feel free* to take a drink from the refrigerator.

first impression (n)   The feeling that one has about a person when meeting or seeing the person for the first time.

My *first impression* of him was very different from the way I feel about him now; at first I thought he was uncaring, but now I know that he's shy.

fitting room (n)   A room where one may try on clothes in a department store.

Because she was unsure what size she wore, Mary took several different sizes of the same dress to try on in the *fitting room.*

fix someone up (v)   To arrange a date for a friend.

Mary offered to *fix Jane up* with a date while she was visiting her in Chicago.

flea market (n)   A market where individual vendors sell a great variety of new and used merchandize.

One can find anything from a used toaster to new wedding gown at a *flea market.*

flu (n)   Short for influenza, a disease which result in high fever, chills, weakness, and muscle ache.

Because I had the flu, I missed four days of class.

forward (v)   To send mail to another address.

The post office will *forward* your mail to your new address if you ask them to.

fun-loving (adj)   Enjoying having a good time.

Marty is a *fun-loving* person; she knows how to amuse herself and those around her.

get a kick out of (v)   An expression meaning to enjoy or to be greatly amused by something.

New parents *get a kick out of* the humorous things their children do and say.

go all out (v)   An expression meaning to do one's best or to provide the highest standard of quality.

When Allen's parents come to visit him in the United States, he plans to *go all out* to entertain them by taking them to Washington, D.C., and to see plays in New York City.

go ahead (v)   To begin; to proceed.

When my mother got on the line, the operator told me to *go ahead.*

go out (v)   To date.

Will you *go out* with me Saturday night?

greeting cards (n)   Cards which contain a message which is appropriate to a specific occasion, e.g. birthday cards.

Valentine's Day cards and Mother's Day cards are two of the most popular types of *greeting cards.*

groom (n)   A man who is getting married.

The *groom* looked very nervous before the wedding ceremony.

hair spray (n)   A liquid that is sprayed on the hair to keep it in place.

Most hairstylists use *hair spray* on their customers' hair to keep it in place.

hairstyle (n)   The way in which a person wears his or her hair.

Some women look better in long *hairstyles,* which seem softer and more romantic.

handsome (adj)   Nice-looking (usually refers to a male).

I think he is *handsome* because he has beautiful eyes and dark hair.

hardware store (n)   A store that sells tools, paint, pipes, nails, and other equipment needed to make general repairs or alterations on a building.

We bought some insulation, a hammer, a screwdriver, and a ladder at the *hardware store.*

have pull (v)   An expression meaning to have influence in a situation.

Because older Americans are frequent voters and control a great deal of wealth, they *have pull* in national elections.

hold one's own (v)   To assert oneself; to take an active part.

Although she was hesitant about speaking in public, she managed to *hold her own* quite nicely.

home remedies (n)   Cures or purported cures that people pass from generation to generation.

Chicken soup is a *home remedy* for a cold, the flu, or an upset stomach.

homesick (adj)   Feeling sad about being separated from one's home and family.

He was *homesick* as soon as the plane left the airport.

honeymoon (n)   The vacation a newly married couple takes after the wedding.

Niagara Falls is a popular spot for people to go on their honeymoon.

house call (n)   A visit made by a doctor to the home of a sick person.

Doctors used to make *house calls;* nowadays, patients must come to the doctor's office or to the emergency room at the hospital for treatment.

Humane Society (n)   An organization which takes care of lost, abused, or unwanted animals.

For a small amount of money, one can adopt a pet dog or cat from the Humane Society.

hygiene (n)   Care and cleanliness of the body.

Good *hygiene* will not only keep you clean but will also help you stay healthy.

ID (n)   A card, usually a driver's license, passport, student card, or credit card, which establishes one's identity, age, and/or address.

Before I could cash a check at the bank, they asked to see my *ID*.

image (n)   The way something looks; appearance.

The *image* of a very tall, thin, muscular man makes me think of a basketball player.

intention (n)   What someone plans to do.

Was it your *intention* to make me angry by ignoring me?

intimate (adj)   Very personal.

I had an *intimate* discussion with my best friend about my personal problems.

landlord (n)   A property owner who rents apartments, houses, or office space to others.

George called the *landlord* to have him fix the leaky water pipes.

lasagna (n)   A popular Italian dish consisting of layers of wide noodles, cheese, meat, and tomato sauce.

Lasagna is one of my favorite foods, even though it's fattening.

lay (someone) off (v)   To cease to employ someone, usually temporarily.

Because the company had lost much business, it *laid off* a dozen workers.

love life (n)   The romance in one's life.

Most people consider the details of their *love life* to be confidential; they talk about them only with intimate friends.

mail order (adj)   A business or the merchandise of a business which allows customers to order goods through the mail by filling out a form or by calling in their order.

When you deal with *mail order* firms, keep a copy of your order and a record of your payment in case you have to return the merchandise.

makeup (n)   Cosmetics that women use to improve their appearance, such as lipstick, powder, and mascara.

Most women look more attractive with a little *makeup*.

make up (v)   To apologize and become friends aagain after having quarreled.

Jim and Sally *make up* each time they have a fight by remembering how much they love each other.

match (v)   To put together two or more items that are similar.

Sometimes it is very hard to find a blouse to *match* a skirt.

mayonnaise (n)   A sauce made of eggs, vinegar, and oil and used on sandwiches and in salads.

When I told the waitress that I didn't want *mayonnaise* on my sandwich, she yelled to the kitchen, "Hold the mayo!"

medicated (adj)   A product that contains some form of medicine.

She uses a specially *medicated* cream to cure her baby's diaper rash.

MTV (n)   Music Television, a 24-hour cable television channel which features videos of popular songs.

On *MTV*, videos create a visual image of the song which helps to publicize the recording.

mutual (adj)   Common to both.

After we talked and compared notes, we found that we had several *mutual* friends and *mutual* interests.

name brand (n)   A well-advertised brand of merchandise which is readily recognized by consumers.

Name brand merchandise is often much more expensive than other brands because advertising costs are significantly higher.

nickname (n)   A special name given to one by family or friends.

The football player's *nickname* was "Steamroller" because of his ability to tackle and to intimidate opposing players with his size.

no-name brand (n) Merchandise which is not advertised and which sells at a lower price than competitive brands which are advertised.

Some people prefer *no-name* brands because they are often equal in quality and are much less expensive than name-brand merchandise.

nonverbal (adj) Without words.

A smile is a pleasant form of *nonverbal* communication.

Odor Eaters (n) Brand name for a product used to absorb unpleasant odors in the shoes.

He bought *Odor Eaters* for his shoes when he noticed that they smelled bad.

one-liner (n) A joke that can be told in one sentence.

Bob Hope, a famous American comedian, is well known for his outrageous *one-liners*.

opposite sex (n) The sex other than one's own.

Shy people often have trouble talking with members of the *opposite sex*.

out front (adv) In front of a building.

I'll meet you *out front* in ten minutes.

overall (adv) Generally.

Although I have complaints about the food, *overall* I would rate the vacation as outstanding.

pair up (v) To form pairs, especially opposite-sex pairs who spend much time together.

In high school, boys and girls often *pair up*.

patient (n) Someone who is under the care of a doctor or dentist.

Five *patients* were waioting to see the doctor.

patient (adj) Not in a hurry.

Be *patient*. Someone will assist you shortly.

perception (n) The way one sees things.

Our *perception* of life changes as we get older.

perm (n) A hair treatment done to curl the hair.

Anna got a *perm* to add curl and body to her hair.

personal questions (n) Questions about things that people do not want to share, such as their income, age, or weight.

Unless you are a very close friend, you should not ask *personal questions* about anyone.

physician (n) Doctor.

What *physician* do you use?

positive (adj) In medicine, a term indicating that the bacterium or virus tested for has been found.

The throat culture is *positive*. You will have to take penicillin for ten days.

posture (n) The way one holds one's body when standing or sitting.

People who stand up straight have good *posture*.

privacy (n) Not being disturbed, staying to oneself.

I enjoy socializing, but I also enjoy the *privacy* of my room. There I can be alone with my thoughts, my music, and my books.

profile (n) Side view of a person's face.

Tom drew a lovely *profile* of Dottie's face.

pushy (adj) Trying to get others to do things they either are not ready to do or don't want to do.

Valerie is well liked because she compromises with people; her brother is not liked because he is very *pushy*.

raffle (n)   A money-raising event where chances are sold to win a certain item.

The prize for the *raffle* was a 24-inch color television.

rain check (n)   A credit from a store to buy a particular out-of-stock product on another day.

You may use this *rain check* next week when our new supply of Aunt Rhona's chocolate cake comes in.

receipt (n)   A paper that shows that you have paid for a product or service.

Because I didn't have the *receipt* to prove that I had bought the shirt in that store, I couldn't return it.

receiving line (n)   A line formed by people being honored at a reception. Guests walk from one honored person to another, congratulating them.

Of the people on the *receiving line,* we knew only the bride and groom.

reception (n)   A party held after an event such as a marriage ceremony.

The wedding *reception* was held at a lovely restaurant.

rest room (n)   Public toilet.

Can you tell me where the *rest room* is?

roommate (n)   A person one shares one's lodging with.

Although some colleges allow you to choose your *roommate,* many colleges assign roommates while you are living in dormitory housing.

seconds (n)   A portion of food offered after the first serving.

Although he was still hungry, he was too shy to ask for *seconds.*

See you later. (v)   Good-bye.

I have to go now. *See you later.*

service (n)   Religious ritual performed at a wedding or funeral.

We attended the funeral *service* at the chapel.

shake (n)   A drink made of ice cream, whipped cream, flavored sauce, and milk, beaten to a frothy consistency. (Also called *milkshake.*)

A strawberry *shake* is refreshing on a hot day.

short cut (n)   A quicker or easier way.

To save time going to class, William took a *short cut* across the field instead of walking on the sidewalk.

showroom (n)   A place where merchandise is displayed.

Because we wanted to compare the prices and features of several models of cars, we visited several *showrooms* before we made our final choice.

shrug (v)   To lift and drop one's shoulders.

He *shrugged* to indicate that he didn't know the answer.

side effects (n)   Complications or problems.

The *side effects* of this drug are sleepiness and dizziness.

singles bar (n)   A bar where unmarried people go to meet each other.

Joan met her husband at a *singles bar.*

snack (n)   A light meal.

In the evening while watching television, the family ate a *snack* of potato chips, dip, and grapes.

socialized medicine (n)   A health care plan sponsored and regulated by the government.

In a country with *socialized medicine,* every individual has access to health care.

stag party (n)   An all-male party, usually given for the groom by his friends before his marriage.

On his last night as a bachelor, his friends gave him a *stag party.*

stereotype (n and v)   A preconceived notion, usually false, about a group of individuals; to judge groups of individuals by preset and often prejudicial standards.

The *stereotype* of a college professor is that of a person who is male, absentminded, and interested in nothing but research.

Until they get to know them, adults sometimes *stereotype* teenagers who congregate in malls as loud, loitering, larcenous pests.

stock (n)   The inventory or goods a storekeeper has on the premises.

We don't have that item in *stock*.

strep throat (n)   Illness caused by the streptococcus bacterium.

She was absent from school for three days with a *strep throat*.

student advisor (n)   A faculty or staff member who is assigned to help students plan their academic programs.

Because Martha was unsure which classes to take, she asked her *student advisor* to help her with her course schedule.

stuffed shells (n)   Large macaroni shaped like shells, filled with cheese and cooked in tomato sauce.

The *stuffed shells* were very tasty.

superstition (n)   A belief in something that is illogical or scientifically untrue.

In the United States, people have *superstitions* that the number 13 is unlucky and that breaking a mirror brings bad luck.

swingers (n)   A group of individuals who are aware of fashion trends and behaviors; individuals who engage in illicit sexual behavior.

The new fraternity members thought they were real *swingers* because they had joined the most prestigious fraternity on campus.

to go (adv)   An idiom used in a fast-food or other restaurant indicating that you will not eat the food in the restaurant but will take it with you to eat it elsewhere.

Give me a cheeseburger, ketchup only, a large order of french fries, and a strawberry shake *to go*.

tongue-twister (n)   A phrase that is difficult to say, e.g., "Peter Piper picked a peck of pickled peppers."

To help with students' diction, teachers sometimes have their students practice saying tongue-twisters like "Sally sells sea shells on the seashore."

top ten rating (n)   Ranking of items, e.g., ten best selling books or recordings.

The novel *Shogun* by James Clavel remained in the top ten rating for fiction for 32 weeks.

traveler's check (n)   An internationally accepted check issued by a major bank or credit institution (e.g., American Express) to an individual who pays for them in advance. These checks are accepted as cash in most businesses but require that one show identification (ID) before the check can be negotiated.

Most business people purchase *traveler's checks* because they are readily accepted for purchases and will be replaced by the issuing institution if they are lost or stolen.

upset (adj)   Feeling uneasy or emotionally uncomfortable.

When I failed history I was very *upset*.

vet (n)   Short for *veterinarian*. A doctor who treats animals.

I took my dog to the *vet* for his shots.

want ad (n)   An advertisement appearing in a publication indicating an article, a position, or a service that an individual wants to acquire.

When I graduated from college, I read the *want ads* in every major paper in Missouri to locate a job opening for a computer analyst.

weekend (n)   Saturday and Sunday; a "three-day weekend" occurs when a holiday falls on a Monday or Friday, thus giving workers Friday (or Monday), Saturday, and Sunday off from work.

Most people look forward to Labor Day and Memorial Day Weekends because on these *weekends,* workers get three days off.

white lie (n)   A falsehood told to avoid hurting someone's feelings or to keep one from getting into trouble.

She didn't want to go out with him, so she told a *white lie:* She said she had another date.

wink (v)   To close and quickly open one eye.

Uncle Tom smiled and *winked* at Mary as he gave her some candy.

you're kidding   An expression to mean someone is joking, or that you don't believe what someone has told you.

When Robert told his sister that he had broken his arm she said, *"you're kidding!"*